The Shorter Latin Primer

The Revised Latin Primer

BY BENJAMIN HALL KENNEDY, D.D.

New Edition, Edited and further revised by
Sir James Mountford
D.Litt., D.C.L., LL.D.

BENJAMIN HALL KENNEDY, D.D.

The Shorter Latin Primer

New Edition Revised by

SIR JAMES MOUNTFORD

D.Litt., D.C.L., LL.D.

LONGMAN

LONGMAN GROUP UK LIMITED,
Longman House, Burnt Mill, Harlow,
Essex CM20 2JE, England
and Associated Companies throughout the World.

© Longman Group Limited 1962

New edition 1962

Twentieth impression 1994

ISBN 0 582 36241 5

Cover photographs by
J. ALLAN CASH

Produced through Longman Malaysia, GPS

*The Publisher's policy is to use paper manufactured
from sustainable forests.*

PREFACE

THE aim of this new edition of *The Shorter Latin Primer* is to bring a well-known and popular school-book into closer accord with the grammatical conceptions which have established themselves since the last edition. As stated by Dr. B. H. Kennedy in his original preface, *The Shorter Latin Primer* was intended to be a simple manual for beginners in Latin, preparatory to the use of *The Revised Latin Primer*. It was, therefore, made in the main identical in its ground-plan and arrangement with *The Revised Latin Primer* in order to facilitate the passage of the learner from one book to the other.

Bearing in mind the convenience of teachers who are accustomed to the older editions and who will for some time to come find copies of these editions in the hands of their pupils, the publishers have desired to leave not only the numbering of the paragraphs, but also the details of pagination, as far as possible, undisturbed. No fundamental change has, therefore, been made in the general plan of the book, and most of the old examples from Latin authors have been retained.

This revision is based entirely on the new edition of *The Revised Latin Primer*, made by Professor J. F. Mountford, of University College, Aberystwyth. The changes introduced by him have been faithfully followed in the smaller book. Attention may be specially drawn to the following points:

The definitions and rules have frequently been rewritten either to avoid positive error or for the sake of greater clearness.

The quantities are now marked in a less haphazard fashion. The principle now adopted of marking all long vowels and no short vowels is in accordance with the best modern practice, and should leave no room for doubt or misunderstanding. The correct marking of vowels involves the marking of those long vowels which, though they were obvious enough in Roman speech, are now called 'hidden'.

While retaining the old numbering of the paragraphs, it has been possible to introduce many changes in the Syntax.

January 1931.   J. W. B.

PUBLISHER'S NOTE

For this new edition of the *Shorter Latin Primer* the typography has been redesigned and it is hoped that users of this standard textbook will appreciate the greater clarity of the modern layout. Care has been taken to retain exactly the same matter on each page so that the new edition can be used side by side with copies of the former one.

At the suggestion of a number of experienced teachers certain small changes have been introduced and these have been carefuily reviewed by Sir James Mountford on whose revision of the *Revised Latin Primer* Mr. J. W. Bartram based the former revised version of the present book.

CONTENTS

SYNTAX

ACCIDENCE

In this book the sign ‾ is used to indicate that a *vowel* is pronounced long, as in mēnsa; it is not used to show the length of a *syllable*.

THE LATIN LANGUAGE

1 The Latin Alphabet contained twenty-three letters:

ABCDEFGHIKLMNOPQRSTVXYZ.

The sounds which make up the Latin language are divided into

    (*a*) **Vowels,** which can be sounded alone.
    (*b*) **Consonants,** which can only be sounded in conjunction with a vowel.

2 The vowels were represented by the letters, **a, e, i, o, u,** and **y.**
The letters i and u were *also* used to represent consonant sounds. Consonant-i is pronounced like *y* in *yet*: consonant-u is pronounced like English w.

In some books consonant-i is represented by j, and consonant-u is still generally represented by v.

3 Quantity of Vowels. Vowels are called 'long' or 'short'. A long vowel takes approximately twice as long to pronounce as a short vowel. In this book all long vowels are indicated by the sign $-$: occasionally the sign $\smile$ is used to mark a short vowel.

All Vowels not marked are short.

The following is approximately the pronunciation of the vowels:

ā (prātum), as *a* in f*a*ther.
ă (răpit), the same sound shortened, as the first *a* in *a*ha!
ē (mēta), as *ey* in pr*ey*, or French *été*.
ĕ (frĕta), as *e* in fr*e*t.
ī (fīdō), as *i* in mach*i*ne.
ĭ (plĭcō), as *i* in f*i*t.
ō (nōtus), as *o* in n*o*te.
ŏ (nŏta), as *o* in h*o*t.
ū (tū), as *oo* in sh*oo*t.
ŭ (cŭtis), as *oo* in t*oo*k.
ў̆ (Lȳdia, lȳra = Λυδία, λύρα), as French u.

Note.—Knowledge of quantities can only be gained by experience: but (*a*) a vowel is long (i) before nf, ns, *e.g.* īnfāns, (ii) as the result of contraction, nīl for nǐhǐl; (*b*) a vowel is short (i) before nt, nd, *e.g.* amănt (except compounds like nōndum), (ii) before another vowel or h, *e.g.* měus, trăhō.

4 Diphthongs. A diphthong (double sound) is formed by two vowels pronounced continuously. The Latin diphthongs are:

ae (portae) = a͡+e, nearly as *ai* in a*i*sle.

au (aurum) = a͡+u, as *ou* in h*ou*se, German H*au*s.

oe (poena) = o͡+e, as *oi* in b*oi*l.

eu (seu) = e͡+u, *é-ŏŏ* pronounced in one breath.

ui (huic) = u͡+i, as French *oui*.

This last and the diphthongs ei (as *ei* in r*ei*n) and eu are rare. The diphthongs are long.

5 Consonants

    I. **Plosives** (= stops, = mutes, with complete interruption of breath).

	Voiceless (hard) without vibrations of vocal chords	Voiced (soft) with
Guttural { (i) velar (formed at vēlum, or soft palate)	q	g
(ii) palatal (formed at roof of-mouth	c, k	g
(iii) dental (formed at the teeth)	t	d
(iv) labial (formed with the lips)	p	b

    II. **Fricatives** (= spirants, with partial interruption of breath).

(i) palatal		cons.-i
(ii) dental	s	(z ?)
(iii) labio-dental (formed by lips and teeth)	f	
(iv) labial		cons.-u

    III. **Liquids** — l, r

    IV. **Nasals**

(i) velar		(ng)
(ii) palatal		(ng)
(iii) dental		n
(iv) labial		m

H represents a rough breathing.

The pronunciation of the Latin consonants was much the same as that of the English, except that

    b before **s** or **t** is pronounced as p; so *urbs*.

    c always as in *cat*, never as in *cider*.

    g always as in *get*, never as in *gentle*.

    Consonant-**i** like *y* in *yet*; so *iūs*.

n before c, g, qu, like *ng* in *sing*.

r is always trilled or rolled.

s always as *ss* in *mass*, never as *s* in *was*.

t always as in *ten*, never as in *motion*.

Consonant-**u** (**v**) as *w* in *wall*.

x always as in *axe* (= ks), never as in *exact* (= gs).

z as *z* in *lazy* or as *dz* in *adze*.

Double Consonants were both pronounced; so *cc* like *kc* in *bookcase*.

The aspirates, ch, th, ph, found only in borrowed words, were pronounced:

ch like *kh* in *inkhorn*.

th like *th* in *hothouse*.

ph like *ph* in *taphouse*.

6 Syllables. A syllable consists of a vowel or diphthong either alone or with one or more consonants adjoining it: e-ram, prā-vus.

INFLEXION

7 An inflexion is a change in the form of a word whereby its relation to other words is indicated.

Inflected words consist of a **Stem** and an Inflexion.

The Stem either contains or is identical with a primitive element called the **Root**.

PARTS OF SPEECH

8 Words are classified as:

I. **Nouns** (or **Substantives**), names of persons, places, things, or qualities:

Caesar, *Caesar*; Rōma, *Rome*; sōl, *sun*; fortitūdō, *bravery*.

II. **Adjectives,** which define nouns by expressing their qualities:

Rōma antīqua, *ancient Rome*; sōl clārus, *the bright sun*.

III. **Pronouns,** which point out a person, place, thing, or quality without naming it:

ego, *I*; ille, *he*.

IV. **Verbs,** which express an action or state:

Sōl dat lūcem, *the sun gives light*; Rōma manet, *Rome remains*.

V. Adverbs, which qualify and limit Verbs, Adjectives, and sometimes other Adverbs:

> Rōma **diū** flōruit; nunc **minus** potēns est.
> *Rome flourished long; now it is less powerful.*

VI. Prepositions, which (*a*) indicate the relation of a Noun, Adjective, or Pronoun to other words in the sentence: (*b*) modify the meaning of a Verb:

> **Per** Rōmam errō, *I wander through Rome*; **ad**sum, *I am present.*

VII. Conjunctions, which connect words, phrases, and sentences:

> Caelum suspiciō **ut** lūnam **et** sīdera videam.
> *I look up to the sky that I may see the moon and stars.*

VIII. Interjections, words of exclamation: **heu, ēheu,** *alas!*

The Parts of Speech are therefore eight:

> (1) **Substantives,** (2) **Adjectives,** (3) **Pronouns,** (4) **Verbs,** (5) **Adverbs,** (6) **Prepositions,** (7) **Conjunctions,** (8) **Interjections.**

9 Nouns, Adjectives, and **Pronouns** are *declined*; **Verbs** are *conjugated*; **Adjectives** and **Adverbs** are modified by *Comparison*.

There is no Article in Latin. Lūx may stand for *a light, the light,* or simply *light.*

10 Proper Nouns are the names of persons or places, as Caesar, Rōma.

Common Nouns are either (*a*) Concrete: vir, *a man*; mēnsae, *tables*; or (*b*) Abstract: virtūs, *virtue*; or (*c*) Collective: turba, *a crowd.*

11 Numerals are words which express Number. They are Nouns, as mīlia, *thousands*; or Adjectives, as ūnus, *one*, duo, *two*; or Adverbs, as semel, *once*, bis, *twice.*

DECLENSION

12 Declension is a grouping of the forms of Nouns, Adjectives, and Pronouns, according to **Numbers** and **Cases**.
Latin has five declensions.

13 The NUMBERS are two:
Singular for one: mēnsa, *a table*; gēns, *a nation*.
Plural for more than one: mēnsae, *tables*; gentēs, *nations*.

14 The CASES are six:
Nominative, the Subject Case.
Vocative, the Case of Address.
Accusative, the Object Case.
Genitive, the *of* Case.
Dative, the *to* or *for* Case.
Ablative, the *from, by, in,* or *with* Case.

Examples of the Cases:

Nominative.	Sōl lūcet,	*the sun shines.*
Vocative.	Sōl *or* ō sōl,	*O sun!*
Accusative.	Sōlem videó,	*I see the sun.*
Genitive.	Sōlis lūx,	*the sun's light,* or *the light of the sun.*
Dative.	Sōlī lūx additur,	*light is added to the sun.*
Ablative.	Sōle lūx ēditur,	*light issues from the sun.*

Note.—Originally there were two more cases, the Instrumental (merged in the Ablative) and the Locative.

GENDER

15 **Natural gender** distinguishes between (1) male, (2) female, (3) inanimate things.

Grammatical gender refers to Nouns, Adjectives, and Pronouns and distinguishes between (1) masculine, (2) feminine, (3) neuter.

Grammatical gender is often determined (A) by the form of the Nominative Singular; (B) by the meaning.

Nouns which are masculine or feminine according as they refer to male or female, are said to be of Common Gender: cīvis, *citizen*; auctor, *author*.

DECLENSION OF SUBSTANTIVES

16 The five Declensions are distinguished from each other by the final sound of the Stem. They differ clearly also in the termination of the Genitive Singular.

Declension	Final Sound of Stem	Genitive Singular
First	-ā	-ae
Second	-o	-ī
Third	{ some consonant / -i }	-is
Fourth	-u	-ūs
Fifth	-ē	-eī or -ēī

17 The Nominative, masculine and feminine, ends in **s**, except in Stems in **-ā**, some Stems in **-ro** of the Second Declension, and Stems in **-l, -r, -n,** of the Third. The Vocative is like the Nominative, except in the singular of Nouns of the Second Declension whose Nominative ends in **-us.**

Neuters have the Accusative like the Nominative in both singular and plural; neuter plural Nominative, Vocative, and Accusative, always end in **-a.**

In the plural of each Declension the Ablative has the same form as the Dative.

18

FIRST DECLENSION

Stems in -ā. The Nominative Singular is a weakened form of the Stem.

Stem mēnsā-, *table*, f.

	SING.			PLUR.	
Nom.	mēnsa	a table		mēnsae	tables
Voc.	mēnsa	o table		mēnsae	o tables
Acc.	mēnsam	a table		mēnsās	tables
Gen.	mēnsae	of a table		mēnsārum	of tables
Dat.	mēnsae	to a table		mēnsīs	to tables
Abl.	mēnsā	from a table		mēnsis	from tables

Declined like mēnsa: aquila, *eagle*; lūna, *moon*; rēgīna, *queen*; stēlla, *star*.

Nouns of this declension are mostly feminine. A few are masculine, as scrība, *a notary*; Hadria, *the Adriatic sea*.

Note 1.—Dea, *goddess*, fīlia, *daughter*, have Dative and Ablative plural deābus, fīliābus, to avoid confusion with the Dative and Ablative plural of deus and fīlius.

Note 2.—The **Locative** singular ends in -ae; the plural in -īs: Rōmae, *at Rome*; mīlitiae, *at the war*; Athēnīs, *at Athens*; forīs, *abroad*.

SECOND DECLENSION

Stems in -o. The Nominative Singular ends in **-us** or **-er** Masculine; **-um** Neuter.

Stem	anno- *year*, m.		puero- *boy*, m.	magistro- *master*, m.	bello- *war*, n.
SING.					
Nom.	annus	*a year*	puer	magister	bellum
Voc.	anne	*o year*	puer	magister	bellum
Acc.	annum	*a year*	puerum	magistrum	bellum
Gen.	annī	*of a year*	puerī	magistrī	bellī
Dat.	annō	*to a year*	puerō	magistrō	bellō
Abl.	annō	*from a year*	puerō	magistrō	bellō
PLUR.					
Nom.	annī	*years*	puerī	magistrī	bella
Voc.	annī	*o years*	puerī	magistrī	bella
Acc.	annōs	*years*	puerōs	magistrōs	bella
Gen.	annōrum	*of years*	puerōrum	magistrōrum	bellōrum
Dat.	annīs	*to years*	puerīs	magistrīs	bellīs
Abl.	annīs	*from years*	puerīs	magistrīs	bellīs

In puer, gener, socer, &c., the **-e-** is part of the Stem. In nouns like magister, the **o** was dropped and an **-e-** developed before the **r**; the **-s** of the Nominative ending was assimilated to the **r** of the Stem.

Declined like **annus**: amīcus, *friend*; dominus, *lord*; servus, *slave*.

Declined like **puer**: gener, *son-in-law*; socer, *father-in-law*; līberī (plur.), *children*; lūcifer, *light-bringer*; armiger, *armour-bearer*.

Declined like **magister**: ager, *field*; cancer, *crab*; liber, *book*.

Declined like **bellum**: rēgnum, *kingdom*; verbum, *word*.

The following have some exceptional forms:

Stem	fīlio- *son*, m.	viro- *man*, m.	deo- *god*, m.
SING.			
Nom.	fīlius	vir	deus
Voc.	fīlī	vir	deus
Acc.	fīlium	virum	deum
Gen.	fīlī *or* fīliī	virī	deī
D. Abl.	fīliō	virō	deō
PLUR.			
N. V.	fīliī	virī	dī
Acc.	fīliōs	virōs	deōs
Gen.	fīliōrum	virōrum *or* virum	deōrum *or* deum
D. Abl.	fīliīs	virīs	dīs

Declined like **fīlius**: Claudius, Vergilius, and many other proper names.

Note.—The **Locative** singular ends in ī; the plural in īs: humī, *on the ground*; bellī, *in time of war*; Mīlētī, *at Miletus*; Philippīs, *at Philippi*.

THIRD DECLENSION

Consonant Stems and Stems in -i. The Third Declension contains:

A. Consonant Stems.

PLOSIVES:
(1) Palatals, c, g.
(2) Dentals, t, d.
(3) Labials, p, b.
FRICATIVE: **s.**
NASALS: **n, m.**
LIQUIDS: **l, r.**

B. Stems in -i.

21 Syllabus of Consonant Stems.

Stem-ending	Nominative Sing.	Genitive Sing.	English
	Stems in Palatals with **-x** *in Nom. for* -cs *or* -gs		
ac-	fax, f.	facis	torch
āc-	pāx, f.	pācis	peace
ec-	nex, f.	necis	death
ēc-	vervēx, m.	vervēcis	wether
ic-	fornix, m.	fornicis	arch
ic-	iūdex, c.	iūdicis	judge
īc-	rādīx, f.	rādīcis	root
ōc-	vōx, f.	vōcis	voice
uc-	dux, c.	ducis	leader
ūc-	lūx, f.	lūcis	light
eg-	grex, m.	gregis	flock
ēg-	rēx, m.	rēgis	king
eg- ig-	rēmex, m.	rēmigis	rower
ig-	strix, f.	strigis	screech-owl
ug-	coniūnx, c.	coniugis	wife or husband
ūg-	*wanting*	frūgis, f.	fruit
	Stems in Dentals drop t, d, *before* **-s** *in the Nom.*		
at-	anas, f.	anatis	duck
āt-	aetās, f.	aetātis	age
et-	seges, f.	segetis	corn-crop
et-	pariēs, m.	parietis	room-wall
ēt-	quiēs, f.	quiētis	rest
et- it-	mīles, c.	mīlitis	soldier
it-	caput, n.	capitis	head
ōt-	nepōs, m.	nepōtis	grandson
ūt-	virtūs, f.	virtūtis	virtue, courage
ct-	lac, n.	lactis	milk
ad-	vas, m.	vadis	surety
ed-	pēs, m.	pedis	foot
ēd-	mercēs, f.	mercēdis	hire
aed-	praes, m.	praedis	bondsman
ed- id-	obses, c.	obsidis	hostage
id-	lapis, m.	lapidis	stone
ōd-	custōs, c.	custōdis	guardian
ud-	pecus, f.	pecudis	beast
ūd-	incūs, f.	incūdis	anvil
aud-	laus, f.	laudis	praise
rd-	cor, n.	cordis	heart

Stems in Labials form Nom. regularly with -s.

ap-		*wanting*	dapis, f.	*banquet*
ep-	ip-	prīnceps, c.	prīncipis	*chief*
ip-		*wanting*	stipis, f.	*dole* (a small coin)
op-		*wanting*	opis, f.	*help*
ep-	up-	auceps, m.	aucupis	*fowler*

Stems in the Fricative, -s, which, except in vās, becomes -r.

ās-	vās, n.	vāsis	*vessel*
aes- (aer-)	aes, n.	aeris	*copper, bronze*
es- (er-)	Cerēs, f.	Cereris	*Ceres*
is- (er-)	cinis, m.	cineris	*cinder*
ōs- (ōr-)	honōs, m.	honōris	*honour*
os- (or-)	tempus, n.	temporis	*time*
os- (er-)	opus, n.	operis	*work*
ūs- (ūr-)	crūs, n.	crūris	*leg*

Stems in Liquids.

al-	sāl, m.	salis	*salt*
ell-	mel, n.	mellis	*honey*
il-	mūgil, m.	mūgilis	*mullet*
ōl-	sōl, m.	sōlis	*sun*
ul-	cōnsul, m.	cōnsulis	*consul*
ar-	iubar, n.	iubaris	*sunbeam*
er-	ānser, m.	ānseris	*goose, gander*
ēr-	vēr, n.	vēris	*spring*
ter- (tr-)	māter, f.	mātris	*mother*
or-	aequor, n.	aequoris	*sea*
or-	ebur, n.	eboris	*ivory*
ōr-	soror, f.	sorōris	*sister*
ur-	vultur, m.	vulturis	*vulture*
ūr-	fūr, m.	fūris	*thief*

Stems in Nasals.

en- in-	nōmen, n.	nōminis	*name*
on- in-	homō, m.	hominis	*man*
ōn-	leō, m.	leōnis	*lion*
iōn-	ratiō, f.	ratiōnis	*reason*
rn-	carō, f.	carnis	*flesh*
an-	canis, c.	canis	*dog*
en-	iuvenis, c.	iuvenis	*young person*
em-	hiems, f.	hiemis	*winter*

A. Consonant Stems (Genitive Plural in -um).

2

(1) Stems in Palatals: c, g

Stem	iūdic- *judge*, c.		rādīc- *root*, f.	rēg- *king*, m.
SING.				
N. V.	iūdex	*a judge*	rādīx	rēx
Acc.	iūdicem	*a judge*	rādīcem	rēgem
Gen.	iūdicis	*of a judge*	rādīcis	rēgis
Dat.	iūdicī	*to a judge*	rādīcī	rēgī
Abl.	iūdice	*from a judge*	rādīce	rēge
PLUR.				
N. V.	iūdicēs	*judges*	rādīcēs	rēgēs
Acc.	iūdicēs	*judges*	rādīcēs	rēgēs
Gen.	iūdicum	*of judges*	rādicum	rēgum
Dat.	iūdicibus	*to judges*	rādīcibus	rēgibus
Abl.	iūdicibus	*from judges*	rādīcibus	rēgibus

So also: f. vōx, vōc-, *voice*; c. dux, duc-, *leader*; m. grex, greg-, *flock*.

23

(2) Stems in Dentals: t, d

Stem	mīlit- *soldier*, c.	ped- *foot*, m.	capit- *head*, n.
SING.			
N. V.	mīles	pēs	caput
Acc.	mīlitem	pedem	caput
Gen.	mīlitis	pedis	capitis
Dat.	mīlitī	pedī	capitī
Abl.	mīlite	pede	capite
PLUR.			
N. V.	mīlitēs	pedēs	capita
Acc.	mīlitēs	pedēs	capita
Gen.	mīlitum	pedum	capitum
Dat.	mīlitibus	pedibus	capitibus
Abl.	mīlitibus	pedibus	capitibus

So also: f. virtūs, virtūt-, *virtue*; f. seges, seget-, *corn*; m. lapis, lapid-, *stone*; c. sacerdōs, sacerdōt-, *priest, priestess*.

24

(3) Stems in **Labials: p, b**

Stem prīncep-
 prīncip-

chief, c.

SING.		PLUR.	
N. V.	**prīnceps**	**prīncipēs**
Acc.	**prīncipem**	**prīncipēs**
Gen.	**prīncipis**	**prīncipum**
Dat.	**prīncipī**	**prīncipibus**
Abl.	**prīncipe**	**prīncipibus**

So also: c. forceps, **forcip-**, *tongs*; m. auceps, **aucup-**, *fowler*; f. trabs, **trab-**, *beam*.

25

(4) Stems in the **Fricative s.**

Stems in -s do not add s in the Nominative Singular, and generally they change -s- into -r- in the other cases.

Stem	flōs-	opos-	crūs-
	flōr-	oper-	crūr-
	flower, m.	*work*, n.	*leg*, n.
SING.			
N. V.	**flōs**	**opus**	**crūs**
Acc.	**flōrem**	**opus**	**crūs**
Gen.	**flōris**	**operis**	**crūris**
Dat.	**flōrī**	**operī**	**crūrī**
Abl.	**flōre**	**opere**	**crūre**
PLUR.			
N. V.	**flōrēs**	**opera**	**crūra**
Acc.	**flōrēs**	**opera**	**crūra**
Gen.	**flōrum**	**operum**	**crūrum**
Dat.	**flōribus**	**operibus**	**crūribus**
Abl.	**flōribus**	**operibus**	**crūribus**

So also: m. honōs, **honōr-**, *honour*; n. tempus, **tempor-**, *time*; corpus, **corpor-**, *body*; genus, **gener-**, *race*; iūs, **iūr-**, *law*.

26

(5) Stems in Liquids: l, r

Stems in **-l, -r**, do not take **s** in the Nominative Singular.

Stem	cōnsul-	amōr-	pater- patr-	aequor-
	consul, m.	*love*, m.	*father.*	*sea*, n.
SING.				
N. V.	cōnsul	amor	pater	aequor
Acc.	cōnsulem	amōrem	patrem	aequor
Gen.	cōnsulis	amōris	patris	aequoris
Dat.	cōnsulī	amōrī	patrī	aequorī
Abl.	cōnsule	amōre	patre	aequore
PLUR.				
N. V.	cōnsulēs	amōrēs	patrēs	aequora
Acc.	cōnsulēs	amōrēs	patrēs	aequora
Gen.	cōnsulum	amōrum	patrum	aequorum
Dat.	cōnsulibus	amōribus	patribus	aequoribus
Abl.	cōnsulibus	amōribus	patribus	aequoribus

So also: m. sōl, sōl-, *sun*; ōrātor, ōrātōr-, *speaker*, carcer, carcer-, *prison*; frāter, frātr-, *brother*; n. ebur, ebor-, *ivory*.

27

(6) Stems in Nasals: n, m

Stems ending in **-n** do not take **s** in the Nominative Singular. Stems in **-ōn, -on**, have **-ō** in the Nominative.

Stem	leōn-	virgon- virgin-	nōmen- nōmin-
	lion, m.	*virgin*, f.	*name*, n.
SING.			
N. V.	leō	virgō	nōmen
Acc.	leōnem	virginem	nōmen
Gen.	leōnis	virginis	nōminis
Dat.	leōnī	virginī	nōminī
Abl.	leōne	virgine	nōmine
PLUR.			
N. V.	leōnēs	virginēs	nōmina
Acc.	leōnēs	virginēs	nōmina
Gen.	leōnum	virginum	nōminum
Dat.	leōnibus	virginibus	nōminibus
Abl.	leōnibus	virginibus	nōminibus

So also: m. latrō, latrōn-, *robber*; f. ratiō, ratiōn-, *reason*; m. ōrdō, ōrdin-, *order*; m. homō, homin-, *man*; n. carmen, carmin-, *song*.

There is only one Stem in **m**: hiems, *winter*; Gen. hiemis, f.

28 B. Stems in -i (Genitive Plural in **-ium**).

(1) Stems with Nominative Singular in **-is**, and in **-er** from Stem **-ri-**:

	Stem	cīvi- *citizen*, c.	imbri- *shower*, m.
SING.			
N. V.		cīvis	imber
Acc.		cīvem	imbrem
Ger.		cīvis	imbris
Dat.		cīvī	imbrī
Abl.		cīve	imbre
PLUR.			
N. V.		cīvēs	imbrēs
Acc.		cīvēs	imbrēs
Gen.		cīvium	imbrium
Dat.		cīvibus	imbribus
Abl.		cīvibus	imbribus

Declined like **cīvis**: m. amnis, *river*; ignis, *fire*; f. avis, *bird*.
Declined like **imber**: f. linter, *boat*; m. ūter, *leathern bottle*.

Note.—Vīs, f., *force*, Stem vī-, is the only stem in **-i**.

	SING.	PLUR.
N. V.	vīs	vīrēs
Acc.	vim	vīrēs
Gen.	—?	vīrium
Dat.	—	vīribus
Abl.	vī	vīribus

29   (2) Stems with Nominative Singular in **-ēs**:

	Stem	nūbi- *cloud*, f.

	SING.	PLUR.
N. V.	nūbēs	nūbēs
Acc.	nūbem	nūbēs
Gen.	nūbis	nūbium
Dat.	nūbī	nūbibus
Abl.	nūbe	nūbibus

So also: mōlēs, *pile*; rūpēs, *crag*.

30   (3) Stems which have two consonants before the **-i** generally drop **i** before the **s** in the Nominative Singular:

Stem	monti- *mountain*, m.	urbi- *city*, f.
SING.		
N. V.	mōns	urbs
Acc.	montem	urbem
Gen.	montis	urbis
Dat.	montī	urbī
Abl.	monte	urbe
PLUR.		
N. V.	montēs	urbēs
Acc.	montēs	urbēs
Gen.	montium	urbium
Dat.	montibus	urbibus
Abl.	montibus	urbibus

So also: m. dēns, denti-, *tooth*; f. arx, arci-, *citadel*; ars, arti-, *art*; stirps, stirpi-, *stem*; frōns, fronti-, *forehead*; frōns, frondi-, *leaf*.

31   (4) Neuter **i-** Stems (with Nominative Singular in **-e, -al, ar**):

In the Nominative Singular of these nouns the **i** of the Stem has been changed to **e** or dropped (with shortening of the preceding vowel).

Stem	cubīli- *couch*	animāli- *animal*	calcāri- *spur*
SING.			
N. V. Acc.	cubīle	animal	calcar
Gen.	cubīlis	animālis	calcāris
Dat. Abl.	cubīlī	animālī	calcārī
PLUR.			
N. V. Acc.	cubīlia	animālia	calcāria
Gen.	cubīlium	animālium	calcārium
Dat. Abl.	cubīlibus	animālibus	calcāribus

So also: conclāve, *room*; sedīle, *seat*; rēte, *net* (Abl. Sing. -e); tribunal, *tribunal*; exemplar, *pattern*.

Note 1.—Mare, *sea* (Abl. Sing. marī, or more rarely mare; Gen. Plur. marum, rare).

Note 2.—The **Locative** Sing. of the third declension ends in -ī or -e; the plural in -ibus: rūrī or rūre, *in the country*; vesperī or vespere, *in the evening*; Carthāginī or Carthāgine, *at Carthage*; Gādibus, *at Gades* (Cadiz).

32 **Iuppiter** (*Jupiter*) and **senex** (*old man*) have exceptional forms:

	SING.		PLUR.
N. V.	Iuppiter	senex	senēs
Acc.	Iovem	senem	senēs
Gen.	Iovis	senis	senum
Dat.	Iovī	senī	senibus
Abl.	Iove	sene	senibus

33 The following rule with regard to the form of the Genitive Plural may be given for practical convenience:

Nouns with a syllable more in the Genitive Singular than in the Nominative Singular (Imparisyllabic Nouns) have Genitive Plural in **-um**.

Nouns with the same number of syllables in the Nominative Singular and Genitive Singular (Parisyllabic Nouns) have Genitive Plural in **-ium**.

(For Nouns with irregular Genitive Plural see Appendix, p. 109.)

34

FOURTH DECLENSION

Stems in -u. The Nominative of masculine and feminine nouns is formed by adding **s**; neuters lengthen the vowel of the Stem in Nominative and Accusative Singular.

Stem	gradu- *step*, m.		genu- *knee*, n.
SING.			
Nom.	gradus	*a step*	genū
Voc.	gradus	*o step*	genū
Acc.	gradum	*a step*	genū
Gen.	gradūs	*of a step*	genūs
Dat.	graduī	*to a step*	genū
Abl.	gradū	*from a step*	genū
PLUR.			
Nom.	gradūs	*steps*	genua
Voc.	gradūs	*o steps*	genua
Acc.	gradūs	*steps*	genua
Gen.	graduum	*of steps*	genuum
Dat.	gradibus	*to steps*	genibus
Abl.	gradibus	*from steps*	genibus

Declined like gradus: m. frūctus, *fruit*; senātus, *senate*; f. manus, *hand*.
Declined like genū; cornū, *horn*; verū, *spit* (Dat. and Abl. Plur. -ibus or -ubus).

Domus, f., is thus declined (rarer forms in brackets):

	SINGULAR	PLURAL
N. V.	domus	domūs
Acc.	domum	domōs (or domūs)
Gen.	domūs (or domī)	domōrum
Dat.	domuī (or domō)	domibus
Abl.	domō	domibus

The **Locative** domī, *at home*, is often used.

35   FIFTH DECLENSION

Stems in -ē. The Nominative Singular is formed by adding **s** to the Stem.

Stem rē-, *thing*

	SINGULAR		PLURAL	
Nom.	rēs	*a thing*	rēs	*things*
Voc.	rēs	*o thing*	rēs	*o things*
Acc.	rem	*a thing*	rēs	*things*
Gen.	reī	*of a thing*	rērum	*of things*
Dat.	reī	*to a thing*	rēbus	*to things*
Abl.	rē	*from a thing*	rēbus	*from things*

Declined like **rēs**: diēs, *day* (Gen., Dat., diēī); aciēs, *line of battle*; faciēs, *face*; seriēs, *series*; speciēs, *form*; spēs, *hope*; fidēs, *faith*.

Rēs and diēs are the only nouns which occur in the Genitive, Dative, and Ablative Plural. Most nouns of this declension are not declined in the plural.

All nouns of this declension are feminine except diēs and merīdiēs, *noon*. Diēs is f. in the singular when it means *an appointed day*.

Note.—The **Locative** ends in -ē.

Rēspūblica, *the public interest, the republic, the State,* is declined in both its parts:

	SINGULAR	PLURAL
N. V.	rēspūblica	rēspūblicae
Acc.	rempūblicam	rēspūblicās
Gen.	reīpūblicae	rērumpūblicārum
Dat.	reīpūblicae	rēbuspūblicīs
Abl.	rēpūblicā	rēbuspūblicīs

DEFECTIVE AND VARIABLE SUBSTANTIVES

36 Many nouns are found only in the Singular, as:

aurum,	*gold*	iūstitia,	*justice*
caelum,	*heaven*	lētum,	*death*
humus,	*ground*	vēr,	*spring*

37 Many nouns are used only in the Plural:

arma,	*arms*	īnsidiae,	*ambush*
artūs,	*limbs*	līberī,	*children*
cūnae,	*cradle*	mānēs,	*departed spirits*
dēliciae,	*pet*	minae,	*threats*
dīvitiae,	*riches*	moenia,	*town walls*
fāstī,	*annals*	nūgae,	*trifles*
fēriae,	*holidays*	nūptiae,	*marriage*
hīberna,	*winter quarters*	penātēs,	*household gods*
indūtiae,	*truce*	tenebrae,	*darkness*

And names of towns, days, festivals: Athēnae, Delphī, Kalendae, *Calends*; Bacchanālia, *festival of Bacchus*.

38 The Plural of some words has a special meaning (sometimes in addition to the usual meaning):

SING.		PLUR.	
aedēs,	*temple*	aedēs,	*house*
auxilium,	*help*	auxilia,	*allied forces*
castrum,	*fort*	castra,	*camp*
cēra,	*wax*	cērae,	*waxen tablet*
cōpia,	*plenty*	cōpiae,	*forces*
fīnis,	*end*	fīnēs,	*boundaries*
fortūna,	*fortune*	fortūnae,	*possessions*
grātia,	*favour*	grātiae,	*thanks*
impedīmentum,	*hindrance*	impedīmenta,	*baggage*
littera,	*letter of the alphabet*	litterae,	*epistle, literature*
lūdus,	*play*	lūdī,	*public games*
opem (acc.),	*help*	opēs,	*wealth*
pars,	*part*	partēs,	*faction, rôle*
sāl,	*salt*	salēs,	*wit*

39 Some nouns have two forms of Declension:

pecus, pecoris, n., *cattle*; pecus, pecudis, f., *a single beast*; plēbs, plēbis, f.; plēbēs, plēbeī, f., *the common people*.

40 In many nouns some of the cases are wanting; thus:

	feast, f.,	*fruit*, f.,	*help*, f.,	*prayer*, f.,	*change*, f.
N. V.	—	—	—	—	—
Acc.	dapem	frūgem	opem	precem	vicem
Gen.	dapis	frūgis	opis	—	vicis
Dat.	dapī	frūgī	—	precī	—
Abl.	dape	frūge	ope	prece	vice

These have full plural with Genitive -um (except vicium).

41 Some neuters have Nominative and Accusative Singular only: fās, *right*, nefās, *wrong*, īnstar, *likeness, size*, nihil, *nothing*.

Nēmō, *nobody*, has only Accusative nēminem, Dative nēminī; for Genitive and Ablative, nūllīus and nūllō (**69**) are used.

ADJECTIVES AND ADVERBS

42 Adjectives are declined by Gender, Number and Case.

They fall into two main classes, A (**43**), B (**44**).

43 A. Adjectives of three endings in -us, -a, -um or -er, -a, -um are declined like Substantives of the Second and First Declensions, O- and Ā- Stems.

Stem	bono-	bonā-	bono-
		good	

SING.	M.	F.	N.
Nom.	bonus	bona	bonum
Voc.	bone	bona	bonum
Acc.	bonum	bonam	bonum
Gen.	bonī	bonae	bonī
Dat.	bonō	bonae	bonō
Abl.	bonō	bonā	bonō

PLURAL			
Nom.	bonī	bonae	bona
Voc.	bonī	bonae	bona
Acc.	bonōs	bonās	bona
Gen.	bonōrum	bonārum	bonōrum
Dat.	bonīs	bonīs	bonīs
Abl.	bonīs	bonīs	bonīs

So also: cārus, *dear*; dūrus, *hard*; malus, *bad*; magnus, *great*; parvus, *small*; dubius, *doubtful*.

Stem	tenero-	tenerā-	tenero-

tender

SING.	M.	F.	N.
Nom.	tener	tenera	tenerum
Voc.	tener	tenera	tenerum
Acc.	tenerum	teneram	tenerum
Gen.	tenerī	tenerae	tenerī
Dat.	tenerō	tenerae	tenerō
Abl.	tenerō	tenerā	tenerō

PLURAL			
N. V.	tenerī	tenerae	tenera
Acc.	tenerōs	tenerās	tenera
Gen.	tenerōrum	tenerārum	tenerōrum
D. Abl.	tenerīs	tenerīs	tenerīs

So also: asper, *rough*; lacer, *torn*; līber, *free*; miser, *wretched*; prosper, *prosperous*; frūgifer, *fruit-bearing*, plūmiger, *feathered*, and other compounds of -fer and -ger. Satur, *full*, has fem. satura, neut. saturum.

Stem	pulchro-	pulchrā-	pulchro-

black

SING.	M.	F.	N.
Nom.	pulcher	pulchra	pulchrum
Voc.	pulcher	pulchra	pulchrum
Acc.	pulchrum	pulchram	pulchrum
Gen.	pulchrī	pulchrae	pulchrī
Dat.	pulchrō	pulchrae	pulchrō
Abl.	pulchrō	pulchrā	pulchrō

PLURAL			
N. V.	pulchrī	pulchrae	pulchră
Acc.	pulchrōs	pulchrās	pulchră
Gen.	pulchrōrum	pulchrārum	pulchrōrum
D. Abl.	pulchrīs	pulchrīs	pulchrīs

Note.—All adjectives in **-er, -a, -um** are declined like niger, except those mentioned under tener. Dexter, *on the right hand*, may be declined like tener, or like pulcher.

44 B. Like nouns of the third declension are declined (1) Adjectives which have two (rarely three) endings in the Nominative Singular; (2) Adjectives which have one ending for all genders in Nominative Singular.

45   (1) Adjectives with Nominative Singular in -is, Masc. and Fem.; in -e, Neuter: Stems in -i.

Stem   trīsti-, *sad*

	SINGULAR		PLURAL	
	M. F.	N	M. F.	N.
N. V.	trīstis	trīste	trīstēs	trīstia
Acc.	trīstem	trīste	trīstēs	trīstia
Gen.	trīstis	trīstis	trīstium	trīstium
D. Abl.	trīstī	trīstī	trīstibus	trīstibus

So also: brevis, *short*; omnis, *all*; aequālis, *equal*; hostīlis, *hostile*; facilis, *easy*; illustris, *illustrious*; lūgubris, *mournful*.

Some stems in -ri form the Masculine Nominative Singular in -er:

Stem   ācri-, *keen*

	M.	F.	N.
SING.			
N. V.	ācer	ācris	ācre
Acc.	ācrem	ācrem	ācre
Gen.	ācris	ācris	ācris
D. Abl.	ācrī	ācrī	ācrī
PLURAL			
N. V.	ācrēs	ācrēs	ācria
Acc.	ācrēs	ācrēs	ācria
Gen.	ācrium	ācrium	ācrium
D. Abl.	ācribus	ācribus	ācribus

The other adjectives like ācer are: celeber, *famous*; salūber, *healthy*; alacer, *brisk*; campester, *level*; equester, *equestrian*; pedester, *pedestrian*; palūster, *marshy*; puter, *crumbling*.

Note.—Names of months are adjectives (agreeing with mēnsis, m., Kalendae, f., etc.): Aprīlis is declined like trīstis; September, Octōber, November, December like ācer; the rest like bonus.

46 (2) Adjectives with Nominative Singular the same for all genders.

(*a*) Stems in -i.

Stem fēlīci-, *happy*

	M. F. SING.	N.	M. F. PLUR.	N.
N. V.	fēlix	fēlix	fēlicēs	fēlicia
Acc.	fēlicem	fēlix	fēlicēs, -īs	fēlicia
Gen.	fēlicis	fēlicis	fēlicium	fēlicium
Dat.	fēlīcī	fēlīcī	fēlicibus	fēlicibus
Abl.	fēlīcī	fēlīcī	fēlicibus	fēlicibus

Stem ingenti-, *huge*

	M. F. SING.	N.	M. F. PLUR.	N.
N. V.	ingēns	ingēns	ingentēs	ingentia
Acc.	ingentem	ingēns	ingentēs	ingentia
Gen.	ingentis		ingentium	
Dat.	ingentī		ingentibus	
Abl.	ingentī		ingentibus	

Like ingēns are declined all Present Participles.

47 (*b*) Consonant Stems.

Stem veter-, *old*

	M. F. SING.	N.	M. F. PLUR.	N.
N. V.	vetus	vetus	veterēs	vetera
Acc.	veterem	vetus	veterēs	vetera
Gen.	veteris	veteris	veterum	veterum
Dat.	veterī	veterī	veteribus	veteribus
Abl.	vetere	vetere	veteribus	veteribus

The most important adjectives with consonant-stems are: caelebs, -ibis, *unmarried*; compos, -otis, *possessing*; dīves, -itis, *rich*; inops, -opis, *poor*; memor, -oris, *mindful*; particeps, -cipis, *sharing*; pauper, -eris, *poor*; sospes, -itis, *safe*; superstes, -stitis, *surviving*.

COMPARISON OF ADJECTIVES

48 Adjectives are compared in three degrees.

(1) Positive: **dūrus,** *hard.*
(2) Comparative: **dūrior,** *harder* (*rather hard, too hard*).
(3) Superlative: **dūrissimus,** *hardest* (*very hard*).

The Comparative is formed from the Positive by adding the suffix **-ior (-ius)** to the last consonant of the Stem; the Superlative generally by adding **-issimus (a, -um)** to the last consonant of the Stem.

Stem	Positive	Comparative	Superlative
dūr-o-	dūrus, *hard*	dūr-ior	dūr-issimus
trīst-i-	trīstis, *sad*	trīst-ior	trīst-issimus
audāc-i-	audāx, *bold*	audāc-ior	audāc-issimus

49 The Comparative is declined as a consonant-stem, with Nominative Singular endings **-ior** *m.f.,* **-ius** *n.*

	M. F. SING.	N.	M. F. PLUR.	N.
N. V.	trīstior	trīstius	trīstiōrēs	trīstiōra
Acc.	trīstiōrem	trīstius	trīstiōrēs	trīstiōra
Gen.	trīstiōris		trīstiōrum	
Dat.	trīstiōrī		trīstiōribus	
Abl.	trīstiōre		trīstiōribus	

50 The Superlative is declined from **o-** and **ā-** Stems, like bonus.

Adjectives with Stems in **-ro, -ri,** form the Superlative by doubling the last consonant of the Stem and adding **-imus.** Words like niger insert **e** before **r** in the Superlative.

Stem	Positive	Comparative	Superlative
tenero-	tener, *tender*	tenerior	tenerrimus
nigro-	niger, *black*	nigrior	nigerrimus
celeri-	celer, *swift*	celerior	celerrimus

Six adjectives with Stems in **-ili** also form the Superlative by doubling the last consonant of the Stem and adding **-imus**:

facilis, *easy*	similis, *like*	gracilis, *slender*
difficilis, *difficult*	dissimilis, *unlike*	humilis, *lowly*
facili-	facilis	facilior	facillimus

Irregular Comparison

51 (1) Some Comparatives and Superlatives are formed from Stems distinct from that of the Positive:

Positive		Comparative		Superlative	
bonus,	*good*	melior,	*better*	optimus,	*best*
malus,	*bad*	peior,	*worse*	pessimus,	*worst*
parvus,	*small*	minor,	*less*	minimus,	*least*
multus,	*much*	plūs,	*more*	plūrimus,	*most*
magnus,	*great*	maior,	*greater*	maximus,	*greatest*

Plūs is used in the Singular only as a neuter noun; in the Plural as an adjective.

	SING.	M. F.	PLUR.	N.
N. V. Acc.	**plūs**	**plūrēs**		**plūra**
Gen.	**plūris**		**plūrium**	
Dat.	——		**plūribus**	
Abl.	**plūre**		**plūribus**	

Senex, *old*, has Comparative senior *or* nātū maior; Superlative nātū maximus. Nātū maior quam ego: *older than I.*

Iuvenis, *young*, has Comparative iūnior *or* nātū minor; Superlative nātū minimus.

Note 1.—Senior, iūnior are **not** used as true comparatives of senex, iuvenis, but with the meaning *old* (*rather than young*), and *young* (*rather than old*).
Note 2.—Dīves, *rich*, has two forms: dīvitior and dītior; dīvitissimus and dītissimus.
Vetus, *old*, has comp. veterior (rare) and vetustior (from vetustus); superl. veterrimus.

---

52 (2) Adjectives ending in **-dicus, -ficus, -volus** (*cf.* dīcō, faciō, volō), form the Comparative and Superlative as if from forms in **-dīcēns, -ficēns, -volēns**.

Positive		Comparative	Superlative
maledicus,	*evil-speaking*	maledīcentior	maledīcentissimus
beneficus,	*beneficent*	beneficentior	beneficentissimus
benevolus,	*well-wishing*	benevolentior	benevolentissimus

53 (3) Adjectives in **-eus, -ius, -uus** are generally compared by using the adverbs magis, *more*, maximē, *most*, with the Positive: dubius, *doubtful*, magis dubius, *more doubtful*, maximē dubius, *most doubtful*.

54 Some Comparatives denoting relations of place have no Positive, but correspond to Adverbs or Prepositions from the same Stem.

		Comparative Adj.	Superlative Adj.
extrā (adv.),	*outside*	exterior	extrēmus, extimus
intrā (adv.),	*within*	interior	intimus
suprā (adv.),	*above*	superior	suprēmus, summus
infrā (adv.),	*below*	īnferior	īnfimus, īmus
citrā (adv.),	*on this side*	citerior	citimus
ultrā (adv.),	*beyond*	ulterior	ultimus
prae (prep.),	*before*	prior	prīmus, *first*
post (prep.),	*after*	posterior	postrēmus, *last*
prope (adv.),	*near*	propior	proximus
(dē, *down*)		dēterior, *worse*	dēterrimus, *worst*

Formation and Comparison of Adverbs

55 Most Adverbs differ from cognate adjectives in having:

(1) **-ē** or **-ō** for **-ī** of genitive singular masc. of adjectives of the first and second declensions.

(2) **-iter, -ter,** or **-er** for **-is** of genitive singular of adjectives of the third declension.

(3) A few Adverbs are simply the accusative singular neuter of adjectives: facile, *easily*.

The Comparative of an Adverb consists of the accusative singular neuter of the comparative adjective.

Adjective		Adverb		Comparative	Superlative
dignus,	*worthy*	dignē,	*worthily*	dignius	dignissimē
tūtus,	*safe*	tūtō,	*safely*	tūtius	tūtissimē
fortis,	*brave*	fortiter,	*bravely*	fortius	fortissimē
facilis,	*easy*	facile,	*easily*	facilius	facillimē

56 Irregular Comparison has corresponding forms in Adverbs.

Adverb		Comparative	Superlative
bene,	*well*	melius	optimē
male,	*ill*	peius	pessimē
paullum,	*little*	minus	minimē
multum,	*much*	plūs	plūrimum
magnopere,	*greatly*	magis	maximē
diū,	*long*	diūtius	diūtissimē
intus,	*within*	interius	intimē

Magis means *more* (in degree); plūs, *more* (in quantity).

Numerals

57 Numeral Adjectives are of three kinds.

1. Cardinals; answering the question, *How many?*
2. Ordinals; answering the question, *Which in order of number?*
3. Distributives; answering the question, *How many each?*

Numeral Adverbs answer the question, *How many times?*

58 Ūnus, *one*, from o- and ā- Stems, is declined as follows:

	SING.			PLUR.		
	M.	F.	N.	M.	F.	N.
Nom.	ūnus	ūna	ūnum	ūnī	ūnae	ūna
Acc.	ūnum	ūnam	ūnum	ūnōs	ūnās	ūna
Gen.	ūnīus	ūnīus	ūnīus	ūnōrum	ūnārum	ūnōrum
Dat.	ūnī	ūnī	ūnī	ūnīs	ūnīs	ūnīs
Abl.	ūnō	ūnā	ūnō	ūnīs	ūnīs	ūnīs

Duo, *two*, is an o- Stem, and trēs, *three*, an i- Stem.

	M.	F.	N.	M. and F.	N.
Nom.	duo	duae	duo	trēs	tria
Acc.	duōs, duo	duās	duo	trēs	tria
Gen.	duōrum	duārum	duōrum	trium	trium
D. Abl.	duōbus	duābus	duōbus	tribus	tribus

ambō, *both*, is declined like duo, but has ō in nom. and acc. of m. and n.

The **Cardinals** from quattuor to centum are indeclinable. Hundreds from *two* to *nine hundred* are o- and ā- Stems: ducentī, ducentae, ducenta. Mīlle (*a thousand*) is an indeclinable adjective; but mīlia (*thousands*) is a neuter substantive, declined like animālia.

In **Compound Numbers** above twenty, the order is the same as in English. Either the smaller number with et comes first, or the larger without et: septem et trīgintā, *seven and thirty*; or trīgintā septem, *thirty-seven*. Ūnus usually stands first: ūnus et vīgintī, *twenty-one*. In numbers above a hundred the larger comes first, with or without et.

Thousands are expressed by putting (1) the numeral adverbs bis, ter, &c., before mīlle; bis mīlle; or (2) cardinal numbers before mīlia: duo mīlia.

Mīlia is followed by a genitive: duo mīlia hominum, *two thousand men*.

59	ARABIC NUMERALS	ROMAN NUMERALS	CARDINALS: answering the question Quot? how many?	ORDINALS: answering the question Quotus? which in order of number? m. -us, f. -a, n. -um.	DISTRIBUTIVES: answering the question Quotēni? how many each? m. -ī, f. -ae, n. -a.	NUMERAL ADVERBS: answering the question Quotiēns? how many times?
1	I	ūnus		primus (prior), first	singulī, one each	semel, once
2	II	duo		secundus (later), second	bīnī, two each	bis, twice
3	III	trēs		tertius, third, &c.	ternī, or trīnī, three each, &c.	ter, three times, &c.
4	IIII or IV	quattuor		quārtus	quaternī	quater
5	V	quīnque		quīntus	quīnī	quīnquiēns
6	VI	sex		sextus	sēnī	sexiēns
7	VII	septem		septimus	septēnī	septiēns
8	VIII	octō		octāvus	octōnī	octiēns
9	IX	novem		nōnus	novēnī	noviēns
10	X	decem		decimus	dēnī	deciēns
11	XI	ūndecim		ūndecimus	ūndēnī	ūndeciēns
12	XII	duodecim		duodecimus	duodēnī	duodeciēns
13	XIII	tredecim		tertius decimus	ternī dēnī	terdeciēns
14	XIV	quattuordecim		quārtus decimus	quaternī dēnī	quattuordeciēns
15	XV	quīndecim		quīntus decimus	quīnī dēnī	quīndeciēns
16	XVI	sēdecim		sextus decimus	sēnī dēnī	sēdeciēns
17	XVII	septendecim		septimus decimus	septēnī dēnī	septiēnsdeciēns
18	XVIII	duodēvīgintī		duodēvīcēnsimus	duodēvīcēnī	duodēvīciēns

19	XIX	ūndēvīgintī	ūndēvīcēnsimus	ūndēvīcēnī	ūndēvīciēns
20	XX	vīgintī	vīcēnsimus	vīcēnī	vīciēns
21	XXI	ūnus et vīgintī	ūnus et vīcēnsimus	vīcēnī singulī	semel et vīciēns
22	XXII	duo et vīgintī	alter et vīcēnsimus	vīcēnī bīnī	bis et vīciēns
30	XXX	trīgintā	trīcēnsimus	trīcēnī	trīciēns
40	XL	quadrāgintā	quadrāgēnsimus	quadrāgēnī	quadrāgiēns
50	L	quīnquāgintā	quīnquāgēnsimus	quīnquāgēnī	quīnquāgiēns
60	LX	sexāgintā	sexāgēnsimus	sexāgēnī	sexāgiēns
70	LXX	septuāgintā	septuāgēnsimus	septuāgēnī	septuāgiēns
80	LXXX	octōgintā	octōgēnsimus	octōgēnī	octōgiēns
90	XC	nōnāgintā	nōnāgēnsimus	nōnāgēnī	nōnāgiēns
100	C	centum	centēnsimus	centēnī	centiēns
101	CI	centum et ūnus	centēnsimus prīmus	centēnī singulī	centiēns semel
200	CC	ducentī, ae, a	ducentēnsimus	ducēnī	ducentiēns
300	CCC	trecentī	trecentēnsimus	trecēnī	trecentiēns
400	CCCC	quadringentī	quadringentēnsimus	quadringēnī	quadringentiēns
500	Ɔ or D	quīngentī	quīngentēnsimus	quīngēnī	quīngentiēns
600	ƆC	sescentī	sescentēnsimus	sescēnī	sescentiēns
700	ƆCC	septingentī	septingentēnsimus	septingēnī	septingentiēns
800	ƆCCC	octingentī	octingentēnsimus	octingēnī	octingentiēns
900	ƆCCCC	nōngentī	nōngentēnsimus	nōngēnī	nōngentiēns
1,000	CƆ or M	mīlle	mīllēnsimus	singula mīlia	mīliēns
2,000	CƆCƆ	duo mīlia	bismīllēnsimus	bīna mīlia	bis mīliēns

PRONOUNS AND PRONOMINAL ADJECTIVES

60 There are the following kinds of Pronoun: (1) Personal, (2) Reflexive, (3) Possessive, (4) Demonstrative, (5) Definitive, (6) Intensive, (7) Relative, (8) Interrogative, (9) Indefinite.

Personal and Reflexive Pronouns are used only as Substantives; Possessive Pronouns only as Adjectives; the others as Substantives or Adjectives.

PERSONAL PRONOUNS

61 There are three Persons:

First: The person speaking: *I* or *we*.
Second: The person spoken to: *thou* or *you* (s. and pl.).
Third: The person or thing spoken of: *he, she, it, they*.

SINGULAR

	1st Person		2nd Person	
Nom.	ego,	*I*	tū,	*thou, you* (Voc. also)
Acc.	mē,	*me*	tē,	*thee, you*
Gen.	meī,	*of me*	tuī,	*of thee, of you*
Dat.	mihi,	*to me*	tibi,	*to thee, to you*
Abl.	mē,	(*from*) *me*	tē,	(*from*) *thee, from you*

PLURAL

	1st Person		2nd Person	
Nom.	nōs,	*we*	vōs,	*you* (Voc. also)
Acc.	nōs,	*us*	vōs,	*you*
Gen.	{ nostrī* / nostrum },	*of us*	{ vestrī* / vestrum },	*of you*
Dat.	nōbīs,	*to us*	vōbīs,	*to you*
Abl.	nōbīs,	(*from*) *us*	vōbīs,	(*from*) *you*

For the Personal Pronoun of the 3rd Person, *he, she, it*, the Demonstrative **is, ea, id**, is used.

REFLEXIVE PRONOUN (3rd Person)

Acc.	sē or sēsē,	*himself, herself, itself*, or *themselves*
Gen.	suī,	*of himself*, &c.
Dat.	sibi,	*to himself*, &c.
Abl.	sē or sēsē,	(*from*) *himself*, &c.

* Nostrī, vestrī are used as *Objective* Genitives: memor nostrī, *mindful of us* (175). Nostrum, vestrum are used as *Partitive* Genitives: ūnus nostrum, *one of us* (173). The oblique cases of ego and tū serve as reflexives of the First and Second Persons.

62

POSSESSIVE PRONOUNS (Adjectival only)

SING. { 1st Person: **meus,**   **mea,**   **meum,**   *my*
       { 2nd Person: **tuus,**   **tua,**   **tuum,**   *thy, your*

PLUR. { 1st Person: **noster,** **nostra,** **nostrum,** *our*
       { 2nd Person: **vester,** **vestra,** **vestrum,** *your*

Suus, sua, suum, *his, her, its, their,* is the Possessive of the
Reflexive Pronoun.

Meus, tuus, suus are declined like bonus: noster, vester, like
niger. Meus has Vocative Singular masc. **mī.** The other
Possessives, except noster, have no Vocative.

63

DEMONSTRATIVE PRONOUNS

Is, *that,* or *he, she, it.*

	SINGULAR			PLURAL		
	M.	F.	N.	M.	F.	N.
Nom.	is	ea	id	iī (eī, ī)	eae	ea
Acc.	eum	eam	id	eōs	eās	ea
Gen.	eius	eius	eius	eōrum	eārum	eōrum
Dat.	eī	eī	eī	eīs, iīs	eīs, iīs	eīs, iīs
Abl.	eō	eā	eō	eīs, iīs	eīs, iīs	eīs, iīs

Hic, *this* (*near me*), or *he, she, it.*

	SINGULAR			PLURAL		
	M.	F.	N.	M.	F.	N.
Nom.	hic	haec	hoc	hī	hae	haec
Acc.	hunc	hanc	hoc	hōs	hās	haec
Gen.	huius	huius	huius	hōrum	hārum	hōrum
Dat.	huic	huic	huic	hīs	hīs	hīs
Abl.	hōc	hāc	hōc	hīs	hīs	hīs

Ille, *that* (*yonder*), or *he, she, it.*

	SINGULAR			PLURAL		
	M.	F.	N.	M.	F.	N.
Nom.	ille	illa	illud	illī	illae	illa
Acc.	illum	illam	illud	illōs	illās	illa
Gen.	illīus	illīus	illīus	illōrum	illārum	illōrum
Dat.	illī	illī	illī	illīs	illīs	illīs
Abl.	illō	illā	illō	illīs	illīs	illīs

Iste, *that* (*near you*), is declined like ille.

64

DEFINITIVE PRONOUN
Īdem, *same*
SINGULAR

	M.	F.	N.
Nom.	īdem	eadem	idem
Acc.	eundem	eandem	idem
Gen.	eiusdem	eiusdem	eiusdem
Dat.	eīdem	eīdem	eīdem
Abl.	eōdem	eādem	eōdem

PLURAL

	M.	F.	N.
Nom.	īdem *or* eīdem	eaedem	eadem
Acc.	eōsdem	eāsdem	eadem
Gen.	eōrundem	eārundem	eōrundem
Dat.	īsdem *or* eīsdem		
Abl.	īsdem *or* eīsdem		

INTENSIVE PRONOUN
Ipse, *self*

	SINGULAR			PLURAL		
	M.	F.	N.	M.	F.	N.
Nom.	ipse	ipsa	ipsum	ipsī	ipsae	ipsa
Acc.	ipsum	ipsam	ipsum	ipsōs	ipsās	ipsa
Gen.	ipsīus	ipsīus	ipsīus	ipsōrum	ipsārum	ipsōrum
Dat.	ipsī	ipsī	ipsī	ipsīs	ipsīs	ipsīs
Abl.	ipsō	ipsā	ipsō	ipsīs	ipsīs	ipsīs

65

RELATIVE PRONOUN
Qui, *who, which.*

	SINGULAR			PLURAL		
	M.	F.	N.	M.	F.	N.
Nom.	quī	quae	quod	quī	quae	quae
Acc.	quem	quam	quod	quōs	quās	quae
Gen.	cuius	cuius	cuius	quōrum	quārum	quōrum
Dat.	cui	cui	cui	quibus *or* quīs		
Abl.	quō	quā	quō	quibus *or* quīs		

66

INTERROGATIVE PRONOUN
Quis, *who? what?*

	M.	F.	N.		M.	F.	N.
Nom. {	quis	(quis)	quid	Acc. {	quem	quam	quid
	qui	quae	quod		quem	quam	quod

In all other Cases singular and plural the Interrogative is like
the Relative.

67

INDEFINITE PRONOUN

Quis, *anyone* or *anything.*

	M.	F.	N.			M.	F.	N.
Nom. {	quis	qua	quid	*Acc.* {		quem	quam	quid
	quī	quae	quod			quem	quam	quod

In the other Cases singular and plural the Indefinite is like the Relative, except that qua or quae may be used in neuter, nominative and accusative plural.

Quis, both Interrogative and Indefinite, and its compounds, are used **chiefly** as Substantives; **quī** and its compounds **chiefly** as Adjectives.

Quid and its compounds are used **only** as Substantives; **quod** and its compounds **only** as Adjectives.

EXAMPLES:

Is quī venit,	*The man who comes*	(quī, relative)
Quis venit?	*Who comes?*	(quis, interrogative)
Quī homō venit?	*What man comes?*	(quī, interrogative)
Aliquid amārī,	*Some bitterness*	
Aliquod verbum,	*Some word*	

8

COMPOUND PRONOUNS

MASC.	FEM.	NEUT.	
quīcumque,	quaecumque,	quodcumque,	} *whosoever* or
quisquis,	quisquis,	quidquid or quicquid,	*whatsoever*
quīdam,	quaedam,	quiddam (quoddam),	{ *a certain person* or *thing*
aliquis,	aliqua,	aliquid,	} *someone* or
aliquī,	aliqua,	aliquod,	*something*
quisquam,	—	quidquam or quicquam,	} *anyone at all*
quisque,	quaeque,	quidque (quodque,)	{ *each one severally*
uterque,	utraque,	utrumque,	*each of two*

Quisquam is used as a Substantive, singular only, chiefly in negative sentences; haud quisquam, *not anyone*; the Adjective which corresponds to it is ūllus.

69 The following Pronominal Adjectives form the Genitive Singular in -īus or -ius, and the Dative Singular in -ī: **ūllus**, *any*; **nūllus**, *none*; **sōlus**, *sole*; **tōtus**, *whole*; **alius**, *other, another*; **alter**, *one of two, the other*; **uter**, *which of two*; **neuter**, *neither*.

Ūllus, nūllus, sōlus, tōtus, are declined like ūnus (58).

Nūllīus, Genitive Singular, and nūllō, Ablative Singular, of nūllus are used for the Genitive and Ablative Singular of nēmō, *nobody* (41).

	SINGULAR			PLURAL		
	M.	F.	N.	M.	F.	N.
Nom.	alius	alia	aliud	aliī	aliae	alia
Acc.	alium	aliam	aliud	aliōs	aliās	alia
Gen.	alīus	alīus	alīus	aliōrum	aliārum	aliōrum
Dat.	aliī	aliī	aliī	aliīs	aliīs	aliīs
Abl.	aliō	aliā	aliō	aliīs	aliīs	aliīs

Note.—In place of the Gen. Sing. of alius, the Gen. Sing. of alter or the adjective aliēnus is used, to avoid confusion with the Nom. Sing.

	SINGULAR		
	M.	F.	N.
Nom.	alter	altera	alterum
Acc.	alterum	alteram	alterum
Gen.	alterīus (or often alterĭus)	alterīus	alterīus
Dat.	alterī	alterī	alterī
Abl.	alterō	alterā	alterō

	PLURAL		
	M.	F.	N.
Nom.	alterī	alterae	altera
Acc.	alterōs	alterās	altera
Gen.	alterōrum	alterārum	alterōrum
Dat.	alterīs	alterīs	alterīs
Abl.	alterīs	alterīs	alterīs

Like alter, but without **e** before **r** in all cases except the Nominative Singular Masculine, are declined—

uter, utra, utrum, *which* (*of two*); neuter, neutra, neutrum, *neither*. These are seldom used in the plural.

VERBS

70 The **Verb** has:

The **Three Persons**—First, Second, Third.
The **Two Numbers**—Singular and Plural.

Six Tenses:
(1) Present, (2) Future Simple, (3) Past
   Imperfect, (4) Perfect, (5) Future
   Perfect, (6) Pluperfect.

Three Moods:
(1) Indicative, (2) Imperative, (3) Subjunctive.

> The Verb Finite

The **Infinitives** (Verbal Substantives).
Three Participles (Verbal Adjectives).
The **Gerund** and **Gerundive** (Verbal Substantive
   and Adjective).
Two Supines (Verbal Substantives).

> The Verb Infinite

Two Voices:

(1) Active, (2) Passive.

The Verb Finite is so called because it is limited by Mood
and Persons; while the Verb Infinite is not limited.

PERSON AND NUMBER

71 The inflexion of a Verb according to Person and Number is effected by adding personal suffixes:

su-**m,** *I am,* am-**ō,** *I love*		su-**mus,**	*we are*
es (for es-s), *thou art, you are*		es-**tis,**	*you are*
es-**t,** *he (she, it) is*		su-**nt,**	*they are*

The Imperative Mood has only the Second and Third Persons Singular and Plural, not the First.

TENSES

72 The six tenses of the **Indicative** represent an action or state as being: (1) Present, Future, or Past; (2) Incomplete or Complete; (3) Momentary or Continuous.

In English, by means of auxiliary Verbs, such differences can be more accurately expressed than in Latin; some tenses in Latin correspond to two tenses in English, of which one is momentary, the other continuous. Thus, rogō, *I ask,* has the following tenses in the Indicative:

Present	Present	*incomplete*	rogō	{ *I ask* / *I am asking*
	Perfect	*complete*	rogāvī	*I have asked*
Future	Fut. Simple	*incomplete*	rogābō	{ *I shall ask* / *I shall be asking*
	Fut. Perf.	*complete*	rogāverō	*I shall have asked*
Past	Perfect } Imperfect }	*incomplete*	{ rogāvī / rogābam	{ *I asked* / *I was asking*
	Pluperf.	*complete*	rogāveram	*I had asked*

The Present, the Future Simple, and the Future Perfect are called **Primary** Tenses.

The Imperfect and the Pluperfect are called **Historic** Tenses.

The Perfect in the sense of *I have asked* is **Primary**; in the sense of *I asked* it is **Historic.**

MOOD

73 Moods are groups of verb-forms which (either by themselves or in relation to a particular context) represent the verbal activity (or state) as being real, willed, desired, hypothetical, &c.

The **Indicative** mood makes a statement or enquiry about a fact, or about something which will be a fact in the future.

The **Imperative** mood expresses the will of a speaker as a command, request, or entreaty.

The **Subjunctive** mood* represents a verbal activity as willed, desired, conditional, or prospective:

istam nē relīquerīs, *do not leave her!* dī prohibeant, *may the gods forbid!*

THE VERB INFINITE

74 The **Infinitive** is a Verb Noun expressing a verbal activity in general, without limit of person or number: amāre, *to love*; amāvisse, *to have loved*; amārī, *to be loved*.

The **Gerund** is a Verbal Noun, active in meaning. It has no plural: amandum, *the loving*.

The **Gerundive** is a Participle, or Verbal Adjective, passive in meaning: amandus (-a, -um), *fit to be loved*.

The **Supines** are Cases of a Verbal Noun: amātum, *in order to love*; amātū, *for* or *in loving*.

The **Participles** have partly the properties of Verbs and partly those of Adjectives; there are three besides the Gerundive:

(*a*) Act. Pres.	amāns,	*loving* (declined like ingēns)	
(*b*) Act. Fut.	amātūrus,	*about to love* ⎱ (declined like	
(*c*) Pass. Perf.	amātus,	*loved* ⎰ bonus)	

* In the Paradigms the tenses of the Subjunctive are given without any English translation, because their meaning varies so much according to the context that any one rendering is misleading.

VOICE

75 The **Active Voice** expresses what the Subject of a Verb is or does: sum, *I am*; valeō, *I am well*; amō, *I love*; regō, *I rule.*

The **Passive Voice** expresses (*a*) what is done to the Subject of the Verb: amor, *I am loved*; regor, *I am ruled*; (*b*) the verbal activity regarded impersonally: ītur, *one goes.*

76 **Deponent Verbs** are Verbs which have (*a*) indicative, subjunctive and imperative moods passive in form but active in meaning; (*b*) pres. and fut. participles, future infinitives, supine, and gerund active in form and meaning; (*c*) gerundive passive in form and meaning; (*d*) past participle passive in form but generally active in meaning.

77 Verbs in the Active Voice and Deponent Verbs are:
   (*a*) Transitive, having a direct object:
      eum amō, *I love him*; vōs hortor, *I exhort you.*

   (*b*) Intransitive, not having a direct object:
      stō, *I stand*; loquor, *I speak.*

Only Transitive Verbs have the full Passive Voice.

THE CONJUGATIONS

78 A **Conjugation** is a grouping of verb-forms. The four regular conjugations are distinguished by the final sound of the Present Stem, which is most clearly seen before the suffix **-re** (or **-ere**) of the Present Infinitive Active:

CONJUGATION	STEM ENDING	PRES. INFIN. ACT.
First	-ā	-āre
Second	-ē	-ēre
Third	consonant (or -u)	-ere
Fourth	-ī	-īre

Deponent Verbs are also divided into four Conjugations with the same Stem endings.

79 The following forms (called Principal Parts) must be known in order to give the full Conjugation.

	Ā- Stems	Ē- Stems	Consonant and U-Stems	Ī- Stems

Active Voice

	Ā- Stems	Ē- Stems	Consonant and U-Stems	Ī- Stems
1 Pers. Pres. Indic.	amō	moneō	regō	audiō
Infin. Pres.	amāre	monēre	regere	audīre
Perfect	amāvī	monuī	rēxī	audīvī
Supine in -um	amātum	monitum	rēctum	audītum

Passive Voice (and Deponent Verbs)

	Ā- Stems	Ē- Stems	Consonant and U-Stems	Ī- Stems
1 Pers. Pres. Indic.	amor	moneor	regor	audior
Infin. Pres.	amārī	monērī	regī	audīrī
Partic. Perf.	amātus	monitus	rēctus	audītus
Gerundive	amandus	monendus	regendus	audiendus

Alongside of Perfects in **-īvī** and derived forms, we sometimes find shorter forms: audiī *beside* audīvī; audiērunt *beside* audīvērunt; audīstī *beside* audīvistī.

Alongside of Perfects in **-āvī, -ēvī, -ōvī** and derived forms, we sometimes find shorter forms, in which **-vi-, -ve-,** or **-vē-** do not appear: amāstī *beside* amāvistī; nōstī *beside* nōvistī; nōram *beside* nōveram; dēlērunt *beside* dēlēvērunt.

For **-ērunt** (3rd personal plural Perfect Active) **-ēre** was often used: amāvēre, implēvēre, audīvēre.

PERIPHRASTIC CONJUGATION

80 The Active Future Participle with the auxiliary verb **sum** forms an Active Periphrastic Conjugation:

amātūrus (-a) sum (eram, &c.), *I am (was) about to love.*

The Gerundive with the auxiliary verb **sum** forms a Passive Periphrastic Conjugation:

amandus (-a) sum (eram, &c.), *I am (was) fit to be loved.*

81 *The Verb Sum, *I am* (sum, fuī, esse, futūrus).

TENSE	INDICATIVE	
Present	sum,	*I am*
	es,	*you* (s.) *are*
	est,	*he is*
	sumus,	*we are*
	estis,	*you* (pl.) *are*
	sunt,	*they are*
Future Simple	erō,	*I shall be*
	eris,	*you* (s.) *will be*
	erit,	*he will be*
	erimus,	*we shall be*
	eritis,	*you* (pl.) *will be*
	erunt,	*they will be*
Imperfect	eram,	*I was*
	erās,	*you* (s.) *were*
	erat,	*he was*
	erāmus,	*we were*
	erātis,	*you* (pl.) *were*
	erant,	*they were*
Perfect	fuī,	*I have been* or *I was*
	fuistī,	*you* (s.) *have* (s.) *been* or *you were*
	fuit,	*he has been* or *he was*
	fuimus,	*we have been* or *we were*
	fuistis,	*you* (pl.) *have been* or *you* (pl.) *were*
	fuērunt,	*they have been* or *they were*
Future Perfect	fuerō,	*I shall have been*
	fueris,	*you* (s.) *will have been*
	fuerit,	*he will have been*
	fuerimus,	*we shall have been*
	fueritis,	*you* (pl.) *will have been*
	fuerint,	*they will have been*
Pluperfect	fueram,	*I had been*
	fuerās,	*you* (s.) *had been*
	fuerat,	*he had been*
	fuerāmus,	*we had been*
	fuerātis,	*you* (pl.) *had been*
	fuerant,	*they had been*

* It is necessary first to conjugate the irregular Verb of Being, sum, *I am*, esse, *to be*, because it is used as an auxiliary in the conjugation of other Verbs.

This Verb is formed from two roots: es-, *to be*, and fu-, *to be* or *to become*. es- sometimes appears as s- (*e.g.* sum); and between vowels -s- becomes -r-, as: eram.

SUBJUNCTIVE	IMPERATIVE
sim sīs sit sīmus sītis sint	es, estō, *be* (s.) este, *be* (pl.)

THE VERB INFINITE
Infinitives

Present   esse, *to be*
Perfect   fuisse, *to have been*
Future $\left\{\begin{array}{l}\text{futūrus esse}\\\text{fore}\end{array}\right\}$ *to be about to be*

essem essēs esset essēmus essētis essent	#### *Participles* Present (*none*) Future futūrus, *about to be* Gerunds and Supines (*none*)
fuerim fueris fuerit fuerimus fueritis fuerint	*Note 1.*—In the Pres. Subj. the forms siem, siēs, siet, sient, and fuam, fuās, fuat, fuant sometimes occur. In the Imperf. Subj. the forms forem, forēs, foret, forent are frequent. *Note 2.*—Some compounds of Sum have a Pres. Participle: absēns, praesēns. *Note 3.*—Like Sum are conjugated its compounds: absum, *am absent*; adsum, *am present*; dēsum, *am wanting*; īnsum, *am in* or *among*; intersum, *am among*; obsum, *hinder*; praesum, *am set over*; prōsum, *am of use*; subsum, *am under*; supersum, *survive*. In prōsum **d** appears
fuissem fuissēs fuisset fuissēmus fuissētis fuissent	between ō and e: prōdest.

82 FIRST CONJUGATION Ā-STEMS

Active Voice

TENSE	INDICATIVE	
Present	amō,	*I love* or *I am loving*
	amās,	*you* (s.) *love* or *you* (s.) *are loving*
	amat,	*he loves* or *he is loving*
	amāmus,	*we love* or *we are loving*
	amātis,	*you* (pl.) *love or you* (pl.) *are loving*
	amant,	*they love* or *they are loving*
Future Simple	amābō,	*I shall love*
	amābis,	*you* (s.) *will love*
	amābit,	*he will love*
	amābimus,	*we shall love*
	amābitis,	*you* (pl.) *will love*
	amābunt,	*they will love*
Imperfect	amābam,	*I was loving*
	amābās,	*you* (s.) *were loving*
	amābat,	*he was loving*
	amābāmus,	*we were loving*
	amābātis,	*you* (pl.) *were loving*
	amābant,	*they were loving*
Perfect	amāvī,	*I have loved* or *I loved*
	amāvistī,	*you* (s.) *have loved or you* (s.) *loved*
	amāvit,	*he has loved* or *he loved*
	amāvimus,	*we have loved* or *we loved*
	amāvistis,	*you* (pl.) *have loved or you* (pl.) *loved*
	amāvērunt,	*they have loved* or *they loved*
Future Perfect	amāverō,	*I shall have loved*
	amāveris,	*you* (s.) *will have loved*
	amāverit,	*he will have loved*
	amāverimus,	*we shall have loved*
	amāveritis,	*you* (pl.) *will have loved*
	amāverint,	*they will have loved*
Pluperfect	amāveram,	*I had loved*
	amāverās,	*you* (s.) *had loved*
	amāverat,	*he had loved*
	amāverāmus,	*we had loved*
	amāverātis,	*you* (pl.) *had loved*
	amāverant,	*they had loved*

Subjunctive	Imperative
amem amēs amet amēmus amētis ament	amā, *love* (s.) amāte, *love* (pl.)

The Verb Infinite

Infinitives

amārem amārēs amāret amārēmus amārētis amārent	Present amāre, *to love* Perfect amāvisse, *to have loved* Future amātūrus esse, *to be about to love*
amāverim amāverīs amāverit amāverīmus amāverītis amāverint	*Gerund* amandum, *the loving*

Supines

amātum, *in order to love*

amātū, *in* or *for loving*

amāvissem amāvissēs amāvisset amāvissēmus amāvissētis amāvissent	*Participles* Present amāns, *loving* Future amātūrus, *about to love*

83 SECOND CONJUGATION Ē- STEMS

Active Voice

TENSE		INDICATIVE
Present	moneō,	*I advise* or *I am advising*
	monēs,	*you* (s.) *advise* or *you* (s.) *are advising*
	monet,	*he advises* or *he is advising*
	monēmus,	*we advise* or *we are advising*
	monētis,	*you* (pl.) *advise* or *you* (pl.) *are advising*
	monent,	*they advise* or *they are advising*
Future Simple	monēbō,	*I shall advise*
	monēbis,	*you* (s.) *will advise*
	monēbit,	*he will advise*
	monēbimus,	*we shall advise*
	monēbitis,	*you* (pl.) *will advise*
	monēbunt,	*they will advise*
Imperfect	monēbam,	*I was advising*
	monēbās,	*you* (s.) *were advising*
	monēbat,	*he was advising*
	monēbāmus,	*we were advising*
	monēbātis,	*you* (pl.) *were advising*
	monēbant,	*they were advising*
Perfect	monuī,	*I have advised* or *I advised*
	monuistī,	*you* (s.) *have advised* or *you* (s.) *advised*
	monuit,	*he has advised* or *he advised*
	monuimus,	*we have advised* or *we advised*
	monuistis,	*you* (pl.) *have advised* or *you* (pl.) *avised*
	monuērunt,	*they have advised* or *they advised*
Future Perfect	monuerō,	*I shall have advised*
	monueris,	*you* (s.) *will have advised*
	monuerit,	*he will have advised*
	monuerimus,	*we shall have advised*
	monueritis,	*you* (pl.) *will have advised*
	monuerint,	*they will have advised*
Pluperfect	monueram,	*I had advised*
	monuerās,	*you* (s.) *had advised*
	monuerat,	*he had advised*
	monuerāmus,	*we had advised*
	monuerātis,	*you* (pl.) *had advised*
	monuerant,	*they had advised*

SUBJUNCTIVE	IMPERATIVE
moneam moneās moneat moneāmus moneātis moneant	monē, *advise* (s.) monēte, *advise* (pl.)

SUBJUNCTIVE	THE VERB INFINITE
monērem monērēs monēret monērēmus monērētis monērent	*Infinitives* Present monēre, *to advise* Perfect monuisse, *to have advised*
monuerim monuerīs monuerit monuerīmus monuerītis monuerint	Future monitūrus esse, *to be about to advise* *Gerund* monendum, *the advising* *Supines* monitum, *in order to advise* monitū, *in* or *for advising*
monuissem monuissēs monuisset monuissēmus monuissētis monuissent	*Participles* Present monēns, *advising* Future monitūrus, *about to advise*

84 THIRD CONJUGATION CONSONANT (AND **U**) STEMS

Active Voice

TENSE	INDICATIVE	
Present	rego,	*I rule* or *I am ruling*
	regis,	*you* (s.) *rule* or *you* (s.) *are ruling*
	regit,	*he rules* or *he is ruling*
	regimus,	*we rule* or *we are ruling*
	regitis,	*you* (pl.) *rule* or *you* (pl.) *are ruling*
	regunt,	*they rule* or *they are ruling*
Future Simple	regam,	*I shall rule*
	regēs,	*you* (s.) *will rule*
	reget,	*he will rule*
	regēmus,	*we shall rule*
	regētis,	*you* (pl.) *will rule*
	regent,	*they will rule*
Imperfect	regēbam,	*I was ruling*
	regēbās,	*you* (s.) *were ruling*
	regēbat,	*he was ruling*
	regēbāmus,	*we were ruling*
	regēbātis,	*you* (pl.) *were ruling*
	regēbant,	*they were ruling*
Perfect	rēxī,	*I have ruled* or *I ruled*
	rēxistī,	*you* (s.) *have ruled* or *you* (s.) *ruled*
	rēxit,	*he has ruled* or *he ruled*
	rēximus,	*we have ruled* or *we ruled*
	rēxistis,	*you* (pl.) *have ruled* or *you* (pl.) *ruled*
	rēxērunt,	*they have ruled* or *they ruled*
Future Perfect	rēxerō,	*I shall have ruled*
	rēxeris,	*you* (s.) *will have ruled*
	rēxerit,	*he will have ruled*
	rēxerimus,	*we shall have ruled*
	rēxeritis,	*you* (pl.) *will have ruled*
	rēxerint,	*they will have ruled*
Pluperfect	rēxeram,	*I had ruled*
	rēxerās,	*you* (s.) *had ruled*
	rēxerat,	*he had ruled*
	rēxerāmus,	*we had ruled*
	rēxerātis,	*you* (pl.) *had ruled*
	rēxerant,	*they had ruled*

Faciō, dīcō, dūcō, and the compounds of dūcō, in the 2nd person of the Pres. Imperative make fac, dīc, dūc, &c.

SUBJUNCTIVE	IMPERATIVE
regam regās regat regāmus regātis regant	rege, *rule* (s.) regite, *rule* (pl.)
	THE VERB INFINITE
regerem regerēs regeret regerēmus regerētis regerent	*Infinitives* Present regere, *to rule* Perfect rēxisse, *to have ruled* Future rēctūrus esse, *to be about to rule*
rēxerim rēxerīs rēxerit rēxerīmus rēxerītis rēxerint	*Gerund* regendum, *the ruling*
	Supines rēctum, *in order to rule* rēctū, *in* or *for ruling*
rēxissem rēxissēs rēxisset rēxissēmus rēxissētis rēxissent	*Participles* Present regēns, *ruling* Future rēctūrus, *about to rule*

85 FOURTH CONJUGATION Ī- STEMS

Active Voice

TENSE	INDICATIVE	
Present	audiō,	I hear or I am hearing
	audīs,	you (s.) hear or you (s.) are hearing
	audit,	he hears or he is hearing
	audīmus,	we hear or we are hearing
	audītis,	you (pl.) hear or you (pl.) are hearing
	audiunt,	they hear or they are hearing
Future Simple	audiam,	I shall hear
	audiēs,	you (s.) will hear
	audiet,	he will hear
	audiēmus,	we shall hear
	audiētis,	you (pl.) will hear
	audient,	they will hear
Imperfect	audiēbam,	I was hearing
	audiēbās,	you (s.) were hearing
	audiēbat,	he was hearing
	audiēbāmus,	we were hearing
	audiēbātis,	you (pl.) were hearing
	audiēbant,	they were hearing
Perfect	audīvī,	I have heard or I heard
	audīvistī,	you (s.) have heard or you (s.) heard
	audīvit,	he has heard or he heard
	audīvimus,	we have heard or we heard
	audīvistis,	you (pl.) have heard or you (pl.) heard
	audīvērunt,	they have heard or they heard
Future Perfect	audīverō,	I shall have heard
	audīveris,	you (s.) will have heard
	audīverit,	he will have heard
	audīverimus,	we shall have heard
	audīveritis,	you (pl.) will have heard
	audīverint,	they will have heard
Pluperfect	audīveram,	I had heard
	audīverās,	you (s.) had heard
	audīverat,	he had heard
	audīverāmus,	we had heard
	audīverātis,	you (pl.) had heard
	audīverant,	they had heard

SUBJUNCTIVE	IMPERATIVE
audiam audiās audiat audiāmus audiātis audiant	audī, *hear* (s.) audīte, *hear* (pl.)

THE VERB INFINITE

SUBJUNCTIVE	
audīrem audīrēs audīret audīrēmus audīrētis audīrent	*Infinitives* Present audīre, *to hear* Perfect audīvisse, *to have heard*
audīverim audīverīs audīverit audīverīmus audīverītis audīverint	Future audītūrus esse, *to be about to hear* *Gerund* audiendum, *the hearing*
	Supines audītum, *in order to hear* audītū, *in* or *for hearing*
audīvissem audīvissēs audīvisset audīvissēmus audīvissētis audīvissent	*Participles* Present audiēns, *hearing* Future audītūrus, *about to hear*

86 FIRST CONJUGATION Ā- STEMS

Passive Voice

TENSE	INDICATIVE	
Present	amor,	*I am* or *I am being loved*
	amāris,	*you* (s.) *are* or *you* (s.) *are being loved*
	amātur,	*he is* or *he is being loved*
	amāmur,	*we are* or *we are being loved*
	amāminī,	*you* (pl.) *are* or *you* (pl.) *are being loved*
	amantur,	*they are* or *they are being loved*
Future Simple	amābor,	*I shall be loved*
	amāberis,	*you* (s.) *will be loved*
	amābitur,	*he will be loved*
	amābimur,	*we shall be loved*
	amābiminī,	*you* (pl.) *will be loved*
	amābuntur,	*they will be loved*
Imperfect	amābar,	*I was being loved*
	amābāris,	*you* (s.) *were being loved*
	amābātur,	*he was being loved*
	amābāmur,	*we were being loved*
	amābāminī,	*you* (pl.) *were being loved*
	amābantur,	*they were being loved*
Perfect	amātus sum,	*I have been* or *I was loved*
	amātus es,	*you* (s.) *have been* or *you* (s.) *were loved*
	amātus est,	*he has been* or *he was loved*
	amātī sumus,	*we have been* or *we were loved*
	amātī estis,	*you* (pl.) *have been* or *you* (pl.) *were loved*
	amātī sunt,	*they have been* or *they were loved*
Future Perfect	amātus erō,	*I shall have been loved*
	amātus eris,	*you* (s.) *will have been loved*
	amātus erit,	*he will have been loved*
	amātī erimus,	*we shall have been loved*
	amātī eritis,	*you* (pl.) *will have been loved*
	amātī erunt,	*they will have been loved*
Pluperfect	amātus eram,	*I had been loved*
	amātus erās,	*you* (s.) *had been loved*
	amātus erat,	*he had been loved*
	amātī erāmus,	*we had been loved*
	amātī erātis,	*you* (pl.) *had been loved*
	amātī erant,	*they had been loved*

SUBJUNCTIVE	IMPERATIVE
amer amēris amētur amēmur amēminī amentur	amāre, *be loved* (s.) amāminī, *be loved* (pl.)

	THE VERB INFINITE
amārer amārēris amārētur amārēmur amārēminī amārentur	*Infinitives* Present amārī, *to be loved*
amātus sim amātus sīs amātus sit amātī sīmus amātī sītis amātī sint	Perfect amātus esse, *to have been loved* Future amātum īrī (**225**)
	Participle Perfect amātus, *loved,* or *having been loved*
amātus essem amātus essēs amātus esset amātī essēmus amātī essētis amātī essent	*Gerundive* amandus, *fit to be loved*

87 SECOND CONJUGATION Ē- STEMS

Passive Voice

TENSE	INDICATIVE
Present	moneor, *I am* or *I am being advised* monēris, *you* (s.) *are* or *you* (s.) *are being advised* monētur, *he is* or *he is being advised* monēmur, *we are* or *we are being advised* monēminī, *you* (pl.) *are* or *you* (pl.) *are being advised* monentur, *they are* or *they are being advised*
Future Simple	monēbor, *I shall be advised* monēberis, *you* (s.) *will be advised* monēbitur, *he will be advised* monēbimur, *we shall be advised* monēbiminī, *you* (pl.) *will be advised* monēbuntur, *they will be advised*
Imperfect	monēbar, *I was being advised* monēbāris, *you* (s.) *were being advised* monēbātur, *he was being advised* monēbāmur, *we were being advised* monēbāminī, *you* (pl.) *were being advised* monēbantur, *they were being advised*
Perfect	monitus sum, *I have been* or *I was advised* monitus es, *you* (s.) *have been* or *you* (s.) *were advised* monitus est, *he has been* or *he was advised* monitī sumus, *we have been* or *we were advised* monitī estis, *you* (pl.) *have been* or *you* (pl.) *were advised* monitī sunt, *they have been* or *they were advised*
Future Perfect	monitus erō, *I shall have been advised* monitus eris, *you* (s.) *will have been advised* monitus erit, *he will have been advised* monitī erimus, *we shall have been advised* monitī eritis, *you* (pl.) *will have been advised* monitī erunt, *they will have been advised*
Pluperfect	monitus eram, *I had been advised* monitus erās, *you* (s.) *had been advised* monitus erat, *he had been advised* monitī erāmus, *we had been advised* monitī erātis, *you* (pl.) *had been advised* monitī erant, *they had been advised*

Subjunctive	Imperative
monear moneāris moneātur moneāmur moneāminī moneantur	monēre, *be advised* (s.)
	monēminī, *be advised*
monērer monērēris monērētur monērēmur monērēminī monērentur	**The Verb Infinite** *Infinitives*
monitus sim monitus sīs monitus sit monitī sīmus monitī sītis monitī sint	Present monērī, *to be advised* Perfect monitus esse, *to have been advised* Future monitum īrī (**225**)
	Participle Perfect monitus, *advised*, or *having been advised*
monitus essem monitus essēs monitus esset monitī essēmus monitī essētis monitī essent	*Gerundive* monendus, *fit to be advised*

88 THIRD CONJUGATION CONSONANT (AND **U**) STEMS

Passive Voice

TENSE	INDICATIVE	
Present	regor,	*I am* or *I am being ruled*
	regeris,	*you* (s.) *are* or *you* (s.) *are being ruled*
	regitur,	*he is* or *he is being ruled*
	regimur,	*we are* or *we are being ruled*
	regiminī,	*you* (pl.) *are* or *you* (pl.) *are being ruled*
	reguntur,	*they are* or *they are being ruled*
Future Simple	regar,	*I shall be ruled*
	regēris,	*you* (s.) *will be ruled*
	regētur,	*he will be ruled*
	regēmur,	*we shall be ruled*
	regēminī,	*you* (pl.) *will be ruled*
	regentur,	*they will be ruled*
Imperfect	regēbar,	*I was being ruled*
	regēbāris,	*you* (s.) *were being ruled*
	regēbātur,	*he was being ruled*
	regēbāmur,	*we were being ruled*
	regēbāminī	*you* (pl.) *were being ruled*
	regēbantur,	*they were being ruled*
Perfect	rēctus sum,	*I have been* or *I was ruled*
	rēctus es,	*you* (s.) *have been* or *you* (s.) *were ruled*
	rēctus est,	*he has been* or *he was ruled*
	rēctī sumus,	*we have been* or *we were ruled*
	rēctī estis,	*you* (pl.) *have been* or *you* (pl.) *were ruled*
	rēctī sunt,	*they have been* or *they were ruled*
Future Perfect	rēctus erō,	*I shall have been ruled*
	rēctus eris,	*you* (s.) *will have been ruled*
	rēctus erit,	*he will have been ruled*
	rēctī erimus,	*we shall have been ruled*
	rēctī eritis,	*you* (pl.) *will have been ruled*
	rēctī erunt,	*they will have been ruled*
Pluperfect	rēctus eram,	*I had been ruled*
	rēctus erās,	*you* (s.) *had been ruled*
	rēctus erat,	*he had been ruled*
	rēctī erāmus,	*we had been ruled*
	rēctī erātis,	*you* (pl.) *had been ruled*
	rēctī erant,	*they had been ruled*

SUBJUNCTIVE	IMPERATIVE
regar regāris regātur regāmur regāminī regantur	regere, *be ruled* (s.) regiminī, *be ruled* (pl.)
regerer regerēris regerētur regerēmur regerēminī regerentur	THE VERB INFINITE
rēctus sim rēctus sīs rēctus sit rēctī sīmus rēctī sītis rēctī sint	*Infinitives* Present regī, *to be ruled* Perfect rēctus esse, *to have been ruled* Future rēctum īrī (**225**) *Participle* Perfect rēctus, *ruled,* or *having been ruled*
rēctus essem rēctus essēs rēctus esset rēctī essēmus rēctī essētis rēctī essent	*Gerundive* regendus, *fit to be ruled*

89 FOURTH CONJUGATION Ī- STEMS

Passive Voice

TENSE	INDICATIVE	
Present	audior, audīris, audītur, audīmur, audīminī, audiuntur,	*I am* or *I am being heard* *you* (s.) *are* or *you* (s.) *are being heard* *he is* or *he is being heard* *we are* or *we are being heard.* *you* (pl.) *are* or *you* (pl.) *are being heard* *they are* or *they are being heard*
Future Simple	audiar, audiēris, audiētur, audiēmur, audiēminī, audientur,	*I shall be heard* *you* (s.) *will be heard* *he will be heard* *we shall be heard* *you* (pl.) *will be heard* *they will be heard*
Imperfect	audiēbar, audiēbāris, audiēbātur, audiēbāmur, audiēbāminī, audiēbantur,	*I was being heard* *you* (s.) *were being heard* *he was being heard* *we were being heard* *you* (pl.) *were being heard* *they were being heard*
Perfect	audītus sum, audītus es, audītus est, audītī sumus, audītī estis, audītī sunt,	*I have been* or *I was heard* *you* (s.) *have been* or *you* (s.) *were heard* *he has been* or *he was heard* *we have been* or *we were heard* *you* (pl.) *have been* or *you* (pl.) *were heard* *they have been* or *they were heard*
Future Perfect	audītus erō, audītus eris, audītus erit, audītī erimus, audītī eritis, audītī erunt,	*I shall have been heard* *you* (s.) *will have been heard* *he will have been heard* *we shall have been heard* *you* (pl.) *will have been heard* *they will have been heard*
Pluperfect	audītus eram, audītus erās, audītus erat, audītī erāmus, audītī erātis, audītī erant,	*I had been heard* *you* (s.) *had been heard* *he had been heard* *we had been heard* *you* (pl.) *had been heard* *they had been heard*

SUBJUNCTIVE	IMPERATIVE
audiar audiāris audiātur audiāmur audiāminī audiantur	audīre, *be heard* (s.) audīminī, *be heard* (pl.)
audīrer audīrēris audīrētur audīrēmur audīrēminī audīrentur	

THE VERB INFINITE

Infinitives

Present audīrī, *to be heard*

audītus sim audītus sīs audītus sit audītī sīmus audītī sītis audītī sint	

Perfect audītus esse, *to have been heard*

Future audītum īrī (**225**)

Participle

Perfect audītus, *heard*, or *having been heard*

Gerundive

audītus essem audītus essēs audītus esset audītī essēmus audītī essētis audītī essent	audiendus, *fit to be heard*

90 Deponent Verb

Ūtor, ūtī, ūsus, *use* (THIRD CONJUGATION)

TENSE	INDICATIVE	
Present	ūtor,	*I use* or *I am using*
	ūteris,	*you* (s.) *use* or *you* (s.) *are using*
	ūtitur,	*he uses* or *he is using*
	ūtimur,	*we use* or *we are using*
	ūtiminī,	*you* (pl.) *use or you* (pl.) *are using*
	ūtuntur,	*they use* or *they are using*
Future Simple	ūtar,	*I shall use*
	ūtēris,	*you* (s.) *will use*
	ūtētur,	*he will use*
	ūtēmur,	*we shall use*
	ūtēminī,	*you* (pl.) *will use*
	ūtentur,	*they will use*
Imperfect	ūtēbar,	*I was using*
	ūtēbāris,	*you* (s.) *were using*
	ūtēbātur,	*he was using*
	ūtēbāmur,	*we were using*
	ūtēbāminī,	*you* (pl.) *were using*
	ūtēbantur,	*they were using*
Perfect	ūsus sum,	*I have used* or *I used*
	ūsus es,	*you* (s.) *have used* or *you* (s.) *used*
	ūsus est,	*he has used* or *he used*
	ūsī sumus,	*we have used* or *we used*
	ūsī estis,	*you* (pl.) *have used* or *you* (pl.) *used*
	ūsī sunt,	*they have used* or *they used*
Future Perfect	ūsus erō,	*I shall have used*
	ūsus eris,	*you* (s.) *will have used*
	ūsus erit,	*he will have used*
	ūsī erimus,	*we shall have used*
	ūsī eritis,	*you* (pl.) *will have used*
	ūsī erunt,	*they will have used*
Pluperfect	ūsus eram,	*I had used*
	ūsus erās,	*you* (s.) *had used*
	ūsus erat,	*he had used*
	ūsī erāmus,	*we had used*
	ūsī erātis,	*you* (pl.) *had used*
	ūsī erant,	*they had used*

Subjunctive	Imperative
ūtar ūtāris ūtātur utāmur ūtāminī ūtantur	ūtere, *use* (s.) ūtiminī, *use* (pl.)

The Verb Infinite

Infinitives

ūterer ūterēsis ūterētur ūterēmur ūterēminī ūterentur	Present	ūtī, *to use*
	Perfect	ūsus esse, *to have used*
	Future	ūsūrus esse, *to be about to use*

Gerund
ūtendum, *using*

ūsus sim ūsus sīs ūsus sit ūsī sīmus ūsī sītis ūsī sint	

Supines
ūsum, *to use*

ūsū, *in* or *for using*

Participles

Present	ūtēns, *using*
Future	ūsūrus, *about to use*
Perfect	ūsus, *having used*

ūsus essem ūsus essēs ūsus esset ūsī essēmus ūsī essētis ūsī essent	

Gerundive
ūtendus, *fit to be used*

91 Many Perfect Participles of Deponent Verbs are used passively as well as actively; as cōnfessus from cōnfiteor, *confess*; imitātus from imitor, *imitate*; meritus from mereor, *deserve*; pollicitus from polliceor, *promise*.

92 Some Verbs have a Present of Active form but a Perfect of Passive form: they are called **Semi-deponents**:

audeō, *dare*	ausus sum	gaudeō, *rejoice*	gāvīsus sum
soleō, *am wont*	solitus sum	fīdō, *trust*	fīsus sum

93 Some Verbs have an Active form with Passive meaning; they are called **Quasi-Passive**:

exsulō,	*am banished*	liceō,	*am put up for sale*
vāpulō,	*am beaten*	vēneō,	*am on sale*
fīō,	*am made*		

94 Some Verbs have Perfect Participles with Active meaning like the Deponent Verbs:

adolēscō,	*grow up*	adolēvī,	*I grew up*	adultus,	*having grown up*
cēnō,	*sup*	cēnāvī,	*I supped*	cēnātus,	*having supped*
iūrō,	*swear*	iūrāvī,	*I swore*	iūrātus,	*having sworn*
pōtō,	*drink*	pōtāvī,	*I drank*	pōtus,	*having drunk*
prandeō,	*dine*	prandī,	*I dined*	prānsus,	*having dined*

95 Inceptive Verbs, with Present Indicative in -scō (Third Conjugation), express beginning of action, and are derived from Verb-Stems or from Nouns:

pallēscō,	*turn pale,*	from palleō
nigrēscō,	*turn black,*	from niger

96 Frequentative Verbs (First Conjugation) express repeated or intenser action. They end in -tō or -sō.

rogitō, *ask repeatedly* (rogō); cursō, *run about* (currō).

97 Desiderative Verbs (Fourth Conjugation) express desire of action. They are formed from Supine Stems and end in **-uriō**.

ēsuriō, *am hungry* (edō).

8

MIXED CONJUGATION

Verbs in **-iō**, with Present Infinitive in **-ere.** In forms derived from the Present stem, these verbs take the endings of the **4th Conjugation,** wherever the latter have two successive vowels. Such forms are given below in **heavy type.**

Forms from Present Stem, cap-i-, *take*

	ACTIVE VOICE			PASSIVE VOICE	
	INDIC.	SUBJUNC.		INDIC.	SUBJUNC.
Present	**capiō** **capis** **capit** **capimus** **capitis** **capiunt**	**capiam** **capiās** **capiat** **capiāmus** **capiātis** **capiant**	**Present**	**capior** **caperis** **capitur** **capimur** **capiminī** **capiuntur**	**capiar** **capiāris (-re)** **capiātur** **capiāmur** **capiāminī** **capiantur**
Fut. Simple	**capiam** **capiēs** **capiet** **capiēmus** **capiētis** **capient**		**Fut. Simple**	**capiar** **capiēris (-re)** **capiētur** **capiēmur** **capiēminī** **capientur**	
Imperf.	**capiēbam** **capiēbās** **capiēbat** **capiēbāmus** **capiēbātis** **capiēbant**	caperem caperēs caperet caperēmus caperētis caperent	**Imperf.**	**capiēbar** **capiēbāris (-re)** **capiēbātur** **capiēbāmur** **capiēbāminī** **capiēbantur**	caperer caperēris (-re) caperētur caperēmur caperēminī caperentur
Imperative Sing.	2. cape			2. capere	
Imperative Plur.	2. capite			2. capiminī	
	Infin. Pres. capere Gerund **capiendum** Pres. Partic. **capiēns**			Infin. Pres. capī Gerundive **capiendus**	

The Verbs whose Present stem is conjugated like capiō are:

capiō, cupiō *and* faciō, fodiō, fugiō *and* iaciō, } and their pariō, rapiō, sapiō, quatiō } compounds,	*take, desire, make,* *dig, flee, throw,* *bring forth, seize, know, shake*
Compounds of speciō *and* laciō { obsolete Verbs,	*look at, entice*
Deponents: gradior, patior, morior, And in some tenses, potior, orior.	*step, suffer, die* *get possession of, arise*

99   IRREGULAR VERBS

Verbs are called irregular which are formed from more than one
root (as **sum, ferō**) or whose tense-forms differ from those of the
regular conjugations.

99a Dō, *I give*, **dare, dedī, datum.**

This verb differs from amō in that its Present and Supine
Stems, **da-**, have a short vowel which is retained in all derived
forms except: **dō, dās; dā** (imperative); **dāns;** and the Present
Subjunctive: **dem, dēs, det, dēmus, dētis, dent.**

100   **Possum,** *I can*, **posse, potuī**

	Indic.	Subjunc.		Indic.	Subjunc.
Present	possum	possim	**Perfect**	potuī	potuerim
	potes	possīs		potuistī	potuerīs
	potest	possit		potuit	potuerit
	possumus	possīmus		potuimus	potuerīmus
	potestis	possītis		potuistis	potuerītis
	possunt	possint		potuērunt	potuerint
Fut. Simp.	poterō		**Fut. Perf.**	potuerō	
	poteris			potueris	
	poterit			potuerit	
	poterimus			potuerimus	
	poteritis			potueritis	
	poterunt			potuerint	
Imperf.	poteram	possem	**Pluperf.**	potueram	potuissem
	poterās	possēs		potuerās	potuissēs
	poterat	posset		potuerat	potuisset
	poterāmus	possēmus		potuerāmus	potuissēmus
	poterātis	possētis		potuerātis	potuissētis
	poterant	possent		potuerant	potuissent

Infinitives: Present, posse; Perfect, potuisse.

Potēns is used as an Adjective, *powerful, able*, never as a
Participle.

101   Ferō, *bear*, ferre, tulī, lātum

		ACTIVE VOICE			PASSIVE VOICE	
		INDIC.	SUBJUNC.		INDIC.	SUBJUNC.
Present		ferō fers fert ferimus fertis ferunt	feram ferās ferat ferāmus ferātis ferant	Present	feror ferris fertur ferimur feriminī feruntur	ferar ferāris (-re) ferātur ferāmur ferāminī ferantur
Fut. Simple		feram ferēs feret ferēmus ferētis ferent		Fut. Simple	ferar ferēris (-re) ferētur ferēmur ferēminī ferentur	
Imperf.		ferēbam ferēbās ferēbat ferēbāmus ferēbātis ferēbant	ferrem ferrēs ferret ferrēmus ferrētis ferrent	Imperf.	ferēbar ferēbāris (-re) ferēbātur ferēbāmur ferēbāminī ferēbantur	ferrer ferrēris (-re) ferrētur ferrēmur ferrēminī ferrentur
Imperative	Sing.	2. fer			2. ferre	
	Plur.	2. ferte			2. feriminī	
		Infin. Pres. ferre Gerund ferendum Pres. Partic. ferēns			Infin. Pres. ferrī Gerundive ferendus	

Forms derived from the Perfect and Supine stems are regular.

102   **Eō** (for **eiō**), *go*, **īre**, **iī**, **itum**

	INDIC.	SUBJUNC.	IMPERATIVE
Present	eō īs it īmus ītis eunt	eam eās eat eāmus eātis eant	I īte
Fut. Simple	ībō ībis ībit ībimus ībitis ībunt		**THE VERB INFINITE** *Infinitives* Present īre Perfect īsse, īvisse Future itūrus esse
Imperf.	ībam ībās ībat ībāmus ībātis ībant	īrem īrēs īret īrēmus īrētis īrent	*Gerund* eundum *Supines* itum itū
Perf.	iī īstī iit iimus īstis iērunt	ierim ierīs ierit ierīmus ierītis ierint	*Participles* Present iēns (Acc. euntem) Future itūrus

In tenses derived from the Perfect stem, forms in **īv-** (*e.g.* īvī, īverō, īveram) exist but are rare. In compounds, -iistī, -iistis are sometimes used for -īstī, -īstis.

The Impersonal **ītur, itum est**, *there is* (*was*) *a going*, is often used.

Transitive compounds of **eō** admit the full Passive inflexion: **adeor**, *I am approached.*

103 Queō, *can*, **nequeō**, *cannot*, are conjugated like **eō** in the forms which occur; the Perfect ends in **-īvī.**

Ambiō, *go round, canvass*, is conjugated like **audiō**.

104

Volō, *am willing, wish.*
Nōlō, *am unwilling, do not wish.*
Mālō, *prefer, wish, rather.*

	INDICATIVE			IMPERATIVE
Present	volō vīs vult volumus vultis volunt	nōlō nōn vīs nōn vult nōlumus nōn vultis nōiunt	mālō māvīs māvult mālumus māvultis mālunt	nōlī nōlīte
Fut. Simple	volam volēs volet volēmus volētis volent	(nōlam) nōlēs nōlet (nōlēmus) (nōlētis) (nōlent)	(mālam) (mālēs) mālet (mālēmus) (mālētis) mālent	Volō and mālō have no Imperative
Imperf.	volēbam volēbās &c.	nōlēbam nōlēbās &c.	mālēbam mālēbās &c.	THE VERB INFINITE *Infinitive* Present { velle nōlle mālle
	SUBJUNCTIVE			*Gerunds*
Present	velim velīs velit velīmus velītis velint	nōlim nōlīs nōlit nōlīmus nōlītis nōlint	mālim mālīs mālit mālīmus mālītis mālint	(volendum) (nōlendum) — *Supines* None
Imperf.	vellem vellēs vellet vellēmus vellētis vellent	nōllem nōllēs nōllet nōllēmus nōllētis nōllent	māllem māllēs māllet māllēmus māllētis māllent	*Participles* Present { volēns (nōlēns) —

The Perfect-Stem forms are regular:

Volu-ī	-erō	-eram	-erim	-issem	{ voluisse
Nōlu-ī	-erō	-eram	-erim	-issem	Infin.{ nōluisse
Mālu-ī	-erō	-eram	-erim	-issem	{ māluisse

105 Edō, *I eat*, ēsse, ēdī, ēsum

Pres. Indic. Act.:	edō, ēs, ēst; edimus, ēstis, edunt.
Imperf. Subj. Act.:	ēssem, ēssēs, ēsset, &c.
Imperat. Act.:	ēs, ēstō; ēstō; ēste, ēstōte; eduntō.
Infin. Pres.:	ēsse.
Pres. Indic. Pass.:	ēstur.
Imperf. Subj. Pass.:	ēssētur.

Most of these forms are distinguished from forms of esse, *to be*, by the long vowel of ēs-.

Fīō, (1) *I become*, (2) *I am made*, fierī.

The forms of fīō take the place of passive forms of the Present stem of faciō, *I make*.

The ī of the stem becomes short in **fit** and before **-er**.

	INDIC.	SUBJUNC.	IMPERATIVE
Present	fīō fīs fit (fīmus) (fītis) fīunt	fīam fīās fīat fīāmus fīātis fīant	(fī) (fīte)
Fut. Simple	fīam fīēs fīet fīēmus fīētis fīent		Pres. Infin.: fierī
Imperf.	fīēbam fīēbās fīēbat fīēbāmus fīēbātis fīēbant	fierem fierēs fieret fierēmus fierētis fierent	*Note.*—When fīō means *I become*, a Fut. Infin. and Fut. Part. are supplied by **fore** and **futūrus**. When fīō means *I am made*, a Fut. Infin. and Gerundive are supplied by **factum īrī** and **faciendus**.

Fīō has no other forms. The meaning *I have become* is represented by sum, *I am*; the meaning *I have been made* is represented by factus sum.

106   DEFECTIVE VERBS

Defective verbs are those which lack a considerable number of forms.

Coepī, *I have begun, I began,* **Meminī,** *I remember,* **Ōdī,** *I hate,* are limited mainly to Perfect-stem forms. Meminī and ōdī, though Perfect in form, are Present in meaning.

Indicative

Perfect	coepī	meminī	ōdī
Fut. Perfect	coeperō	meminerō	ōderō
Pluperfect	coeperam	memineram	ōderam

Subjunctive

Perfect	coeperim	meminerim	ōderim
Pluperfect	coepissem	meminissem	ōdissem

Infinitive, Imperative, Participles

Perfect Infinitive	coepisse	meminisse	ōdisse
Fut. Infinitive	coeptūrus esse	*none*	ōsūrus esse
Imperative	*none*	mementō mementōte } *none*	
Perfect Participle	coeptus	*none*	ōsus, *hating*
Fut. Participle	coeptūrus	*none*	ōsūrus

Note 1.—Coepī has also Perf. Passive forms: **coeptus sum,** &c., which are used mainly when coepī governs a passive infinitive, as: urbs aedificārī coepta est, *the city began to be built.*
Note 2.—Incipiō, *I begin,* supplies the present-stem forms which coepī lacks.
Note 3.—The participle ōsus is active and present in meaning.

Nōvī (Perfect of nōscō, *I get to know*) means *I have got to know, I know;* nōverō, *I shall know;* nōveram (nōram), *I knew;* nōvisse (nōsse), *to know,* &c.

Aiō, *I say* or *affirm*:

Ind. Pres.   **aiō, ais, ait, — — aiunt**
Imperf.   **aiēbam, aiēbās, aiēbat, aiēbāmus, aiēbātis, aiēbant**
Subj. Pres.   **—   —   aiat,   —   —   aiant**
Participle   **aiēns**

Inquam, *I say*:

Ind. Pres. **inquam, inquis, inquit, inquimus, inquitis, inquiunt**
Imperf.   **—   —   inquiēbat   —   —   inquiēbant**
Fut. Simple **—   inquiēs, inquiet**
Perf.   **inquīstī, inquit**
Imper.   **inque   —**

107   IMPERSONAL VERBS

Impersonal Verbs have only the Third Personal Singular of each tense, an Infinitive, and a Gerund. They do not have a personal Subject in the Nominative.

The principal are the following:

Present		Perfect	Infinitive
miseret,	*it moves to pity*	miseruit	miserēre
piget,	*it vexes*	piguit	pigēre
paenitet,	*it repents*	paenituit	paenitēre
pudet,	*it shames*	puduit	pudēre
taedet,	*it wearies*	taeduit	taedēre
decet,	*it is becoming*	decuit	decēre
dēdecet,	*it is unbecoming*	dēdecuit	dēdecēre
libet,	*it pleases*	libuit	libēre
licet,	*it is lawful*	licuit	licēre
oportet,	*it behoves*	oportuit	oportēre
rēfert,	*it concerns*	rētulit	rēferre

108 Some Impersonals express change of weather and time:

fulgurat,	*it lightens*	**tonat,**	*it thunders*
ningit,	*it snows*	**lūcēscit,**	*it dawns*
pluit,	*it rains*	**vesperāscit,**	*it grows late*

Interest, *it concerns,* is used impersonally (**190-193**), though intersum also has all the personal forms.

Intransitive Verbs also are used impersonally in the Passive: **ītur,** *one goes, a journey is made.*

109

TABLE OF PRINCIPAL PARTS OF VERBS*

Present	*Infin.*	*Perfect*	*Supine*

First Conjugation: Ā- Stems

Usual Form

amō	amāre	amāvī	amātum	

Exceptions

PERFECT in -uī:

secō	-āre	secuī	sectum	*cut*
sonō	-āre	sonuī	—	*sound*
vetō	-āre	vetuī	vetitum	*forbid*

PERFECT with **Reduplication**:

stō	-āre	stetī ⎱ -stitī ⎰	statum	*stand*

PERFECT with **Lengthened Vowel**:

iuvō	-āre	iūvī	iūtum	*help*

110

Second Conjugation: Ē- Stems

Usual Forms

moneō	monēre	monuī	monitum	

Exceptions

PERFECT in -uī; but SUPINE in -tum or -sum:

cēnseō	-ēre	cēnsuī	cēnsum	*deem, vote*
doceō	-ēre	docuī	doctum	*teach*

PERFECT in -vī:

fleō	-ēre	flēvī	flētum	*weep*

PERFECT in -sī:

ardeō	-ēre	arsī	—	*burn* (intr.)
augeō	-ēre	auxī	auctum	*increase* (tr.)
fulgeō	-ēre	fulsī	—	*shine*
haereō	-ēre	haesī	—	*stick*
iubeō	-ēre	iussī	iussum	*command*
maneō	-ēre	mānsī	mānsum	*remain*
rīdeō	-ēre	rīsī	rīsum	*laugh*
suādeō	-ēre	suāsī	suāsum	*advise*

PERFECT with **Reduplication**:

mordeō	-ēre	momordī	morsum	*bite*
pendeō	-ēre	pependī	—	*hang* (intr.)

* Forms printed with a hyphen, as -stitī, are used only in compounds.

PERFECT with **Lengthened Vowel**:

Present	Infin.	Perfect	Supine	
caveō	-ēre	cāvī	cautum	*beware*
foveō	-ēre	fōvī	fōtum	*cherish*
moveō	-ēre	mōvī	mōtum	*move* (tr.)
sedeō	-ēre	sēdī	sessum	*sit*
videō	-ēre	vīdī	vīsum	*see*

111   Third Conjugation: Consonant and U- Stems

Consonant Stems

PERFECT in -sī, and SUPINE in -tum:

cingō	-ere	cīnxī	cīnctum	*surround*
dīcō	-ere	dīxī	dictum	*say*
dūcō	-ere	dūxī	ductum	*lead*
fingō	-ere	fīnxī	fictum	*feign*
gerō	-ere	gessī	gestum	*carry on*
intellegō	-ere	intellēxī	intellēctum	*understand*
iungō	-ere	iūnxī	iūnctum	*join, attach*
nūbō	-ere	nūpsī	nūptum	*marry*
regō	-ere	rēxī	rēctum	*rule*
scrībō	-ere	scrīpsī	scrīptum	*write*
sūmō	-ere	sūmpsī	sūmptum	*take*
surgō	-ere	surrēxī	surrēctum	*arise*
tegō	-ere	tēxī	tēctum	*cover*
trahō	-ere	trāxī	tractum	*draw*
vehō	-ere	vēxī	vectum	*carry*
vīvō	-ere	vīxī	vīctum	*live*

PERFECT in -sī, and SUPINE in -sum:

cēdō	-ere	cessī	cessum	*yield*
claudō	-ere	clausī	clausum	*shut*
dīvidō	-ere	dīvīsī	dīvīsum	*divide*
fīgō	-ere	fīxī	fīxum	*fix*
flectō	-ere	flexī	flexum	*bend* (tr.)
lūdō	-ere	lūsī	lūsum	*play*
mittō	-ere	mīsī	missum	*send*
premō	-ere	pressī	pressum	*press* (tr.)
spargō	-ere	sparsī	sparsum	*sprinkle*

PERFECT in -vī:

serō	-ere	sēvī	satum	*sow*
spernō	-ere	sprēvī	sprētum	*despise*
cognōscō	-ere	cognōvī	cognitum	*get to know*
crēscō	-ere	crēvī	crētum	*grow*
nōscō	-ere	nōvī	nōtum	*get to know*

PERFECT in -īvī:

quaerō	-ere	quaesīvī	quaesītum	*seek*

PERFECT in -ui:

Present	Infin.	Perfect	Supine	
colō	-ere	coluī	cultum	*till, worship*
cumbō	-ere	-cubuī	cubitum	*lie*
pōnō	-ere	posuī	positum	*place*

PERFECT with **Reduplication**:

addō	-ere	addidī	additum	*add*
canō	-ere	cecinī	cantum	*sing*
discō	-ere	didicī	—	*learn*
tangō	-ere	tetigī	tāctum	*touch*
tendō	-ere	tetendī	tentum (tēnsum)	*stretch*

Note.—Like addō are most other compounds of dō: *e.g.* crēdō, *believe*; trādō, *deliver*.

PERFECT with **Lengthened Vowel**:

agō	-ere	ēgī	āctum	*do*
emō	-ere	ēmī	ēmptum	*buy*
frangō	-ere	frēgī	frāctum	*break* (tr.)
fundō	-ere	fūdī	fūsum	*pour* (tr.)
legō	-ere	lēgī	lēctum	*choose, read*
rumpō	-ere	rūpī	ruptum	*break* (tr.)
vincō	-ere	vīcī	victum	*conquer*

PERFECT in -ī (without **Reduplication** or **Lengthening**):

bibō	-ere	bibī	—	*drink*
solvō	-ere	solvī	solūtum	*loose*
vertō	-ere	vertī	versum	*turn* (tr.)
volvō	-ere	volvī	volūtum	*roll* (tr.)

VERBS in -uō:

induō	-ere	induī	indūtum	*put on*
statuō	-ere	statuī	statūtum	*set up*

Mixed Conjugation

capiō	-ere	cēpī	captum	*take*
-cutiō	-ere	-cussī	-cussum	*shake*
faciō	-ere	fēcī	factum	*do*
fugiō	-ere	fūgī	—	*flee*
iaciō	-ere	iēcī	iactum	*hurl*
pariō	-ere	peperī	partum	*bring forth*
rapiō	-ere	rapuī	raptum	*snatch*

112   Fourth Conjugation: Ī- Stems

Usual Form

audiō	audīre	audīvī	audītum

Exceptions

PERFECT in -īvī; but SUPINE in -tum:

sepeliō	-īre	sepelīvī	sepultum	*bury*

PERFECT in -uī:

aperiō	-īre	aperuī	apertum	*open* (tr.)

PERFECT in -sī:

hauriō	-īre	hausī	haustum	*drain*
sentiō	-īre	sēnsī	sēnsum	*feel*
vinciō	-īre	vīnxī	vīnctum	*bind*

PERFECT in -ī:

reperiō	-īre	repperī	repertum	*discover*
veniō	-īre	vēnī	ventum	*come*

DEPONENT AND SEMI-DEPONENT VERBS

113   Second Conjugation: Ē- Stems (Perfect -itus sum).

Exceptions

fateor	-ērī	fassus sum	*confess*
reor	-ērī	ratus sum	*think*

114   SEMI-DEPONENT:

audeō	-ēre	ausus sum	—	*dare*
soleō	-ēre	solitus sum	—	*be wont*

115   Third and Mixed Conjugations (Perfect -tus *or* -sus sum).

fungor	-ī	fūnctus sum	*perform*
īrāscor	-ī	īrātus sum	*be angry*
loquor	-ī	locūtus sum	*speak*
morior	-ī	mortuus sum	*die*
nāscor	-ī	nātus sum	*be born*
patior	-ī	passus sum	*suffer*
proficīscor	-ī	profectus sum	*set out*
queror	-ī	questus sum	*complain*
sequor	-ī	secūtus sum	*follow*
ūtor	-ī	ūsus sum	*use*

116   Fourth Conjugation: Ī- Stems (Perfect -ītus sum).

Exceptions

experior	-īrī	expertus sum	*try*
ordior	-īrī	orsus sum	*begin*
orior	-īrī	ortus sum	*arise*
potior	-īrī	potītus sum	*acquire*

SYNTAX

INTRODUCTORY OUTLINE

17 SYNTAX treats of the use of words in the structure of Sentences.

Sentences are either **Simple, Compound,** or **Complex.**

A **Simple** Sentence is one which contains only one Finite Verb. A **Compound** Sentence consists of two or more Simple Sentences linked by **et,** *and,* etc. A **Complex** Sentence consists of a Principal Sentence and one or more Subordinate Clauses **(236-244).**

18 A Simple Sentence has two parts:

1. The Subject: indicating that which performs the action or is in the state referred to in the Predicate.
2. The Predicate: indicating the action or state of the Subject.

19 1. The **Subject** is generally a **Substantive,** or some word or words taking the place of a Substantive:

A **Substantive:** lēx, *the law*; satis temporis, *enough time.*

A **Pronoun:** ego, *I*; nōs, *we.*

An **Adjective, Participle,** or **Adjectival Pronoun:** Rōmānus, *a Roman*; īrātus, *an angry man*; ille, *that* (*man*).

A **Verb Noun Infinitive:** nāvigāre, *to sail* or *sailing.*

20 2. The **Predicate,** since it indicates an action or a state, is a **Verb** or contains a Verb.

EXAMPLES OF THE SIMPLE SENTENCE

Subject	Predicate	Subject	Predicate
Lēx	iubet.	Nōs	pārēmus.
Law	*commands.*	*We*	*obey.*
Nāvigāre	dēlectat.	Satis temporis	datur.
Sailing	*delights.*	*Enough time*	*is given.*

A single Verb may be a sentence. Vēnī, vīdī, vīcī, *I came, I saw, I conquered,* comprises three sentences.

121 Some Verbs cannot by themselves form complete Predicates.
The Verb **sum** is a complete Predicate only when it means *I exist*:

Seges	est	ubi	Trōia	fuit.	OVID.
Corn	*is*	*where*	*Troy*	*was.*	

More often **sum** links the Subject with the **Complement,** which
defines the action, state, or quality of the Subject.

122 Verbs which link a Subject and Complement are called **Copulative Verbs.** Others besides **sum** are:

appāreō, *appear;*   audiō, *am called;* maneō, *remain;*
ēvādō, exsistō, *turn out;*   videor, *seem.*

The Passives of Verbs of *making, saying, thinking, choosing,
showing* (**Factitive** Verbs [134]) are also used as Copulative Verbs:

fīō, *become* or *am made;*   feror, *am reported;*
appellor, *am called;*   legor, *am chosen;*
creor, *am created;*   putor, *am thought;*
dēclāror, *am declared;*   vocor, *am called.*

123 The Complement is in the same case as the Subject.
The Complement may be an Adjective or a Substantive.

Subject	Predicate	
	Copulative Verb	*Complement*
1. Leō	est	validus.
The lion	*is*	*strong.*
2. Illī	appellantur	philosophī.
They	*are called*	*philosophers.*

124 Many Verbs usually require as their object another Verb in the
Infinitive to make a complete Predicate; such are: soleō, *am
wont;* possum, *am able.*

Solet legere.   Possum īre.
He is wont to read.   *I am able to go.*

The Infinitive following such Verbs is sometimes called
Prolative (214), because it carries on (prōfert) their construction.

AGREEMENT

RULES OF THE FOUR CONCORDS

125 I. A Verb agrees with its Subject in Number and Person:

Tempus·fugit.   Nōs amāmur.
Time flies.   *We are loved.*

126 II. An Adjective or Participle agrees in Gender, Number, and Case with the Substantive it qualifies:

Vir bonus bonam uxōrem habet.
The good man has a good wife.

Vērae amīcitiae sempiternae sunt.   CICERO.
True friendships are everlasting.

127 III. When a Substantive or Pronoun is followed by another Substantive, so that the second explains or describes the first, and has the same relation to the rest of the sentence, the second Noun agrees in Case with the first, and is said to be in Apposition to it:

Nōs līberī patrem Lollium imitābimur.
We children will imitate our father Lollius.

Procās, rēx Albānōrum, duōs fīliōs, Numitōrem et Amūlium, habuit. LIVY.
Procas, king of the Albans, had two sons, Numitor and Amulius.

128 IV. The Relative **quī, quae, quod,** agrees with its Antecedent in Gender, Number, and Person; in Case it takes its construction from its own clause:

Amō tē, māter, quae mē amās.
I love you, mother, who love me.

Quis hic est homō quem ante aedēs videō?   PLAUTUS.
Who is this man whom I see before the house?

Arborēs multās serit agricola, quārum frūctūs nōn adspiciet.   CICERO.
The farmer plants many trees, of which he will not see the fruit.

129   COMPOSITE SUBJECT AND PREDICATE

1. When the Subject consists of two or more Nouns, the Verb and Predicative Adjectives are usually in the Plural:

> Aetās, metus, magister eum cohibēbant. TERENCE.
> *Age, fear, and a tutor were restraining him.*
> Venēnō absūmptī sunt Hannibal et Philopoemēn. LIVY.
> *Hannibal and Philopoemen were cut off by poison.*

2. If a Composite Subject comprises different Persons, the Verb agrees with the First Person rather than the Second or Third; with the Second rather than the Third:

> Sī tū et Tullia valētis, ego et Cicerō valēmus. CICERO.
> *If you and Tullia are well, I and Cicero are well.*

3. When the Nouns of the Subject differ in Gender, an Adjective in the Predicate agrees with the Masculine rather than with the Feminine:

> Rēx rēgiaque classis ūnā profectī. LIVY.
> *The king and the royal fleet set out together.*

4. If the Subject refers to inanimate things, an Adjective in the Predicate is generally Neuter:

> Rēgna, honōrēs, dīvitiae, cadūca et incerta sunt. CICERO.
> *Kingdoms, honours, riches, are frail and fickle things.*

THE CASES

THE NOMINATIVE AND VOCATIVE CASES

130 The Subject of a Finite Verb is in the Nominative Case:

> Annī fugiunt.   Lābitur aetās. OVID.
> *Years flee.*   *Time glides away.*

131 The Complement of a Finite Copulative Verb is in the Nominative Case:

> Cicerō dēclārātus est cōnsul. CICERO.
> *Cicero was declared consul.*

132 The Vocative stands apart from the construction of the sentence with or without an Interjection (233):

> Ō sōl pulcher, ō laudande! HORACE.
> *O beauteous sun, worthy of praise!*
> Pompēī, meōrum prīme sodālium! HORACE.
> *O Pompeius, earliest of my comrades!*

THE ACCUSITIVE CASE

Accusative of Direct Object

133 The Direct Object of a Transitive Verb is in the Accusative Case:

> Haec studia adulēscentiam alunt, senectūtem oblectant. CICERO.
> *These studies nurture youth, and delight old age.*

134 Factitive Verbs (verbs of *making*, *saying*, *thinking*, *choosing*, *showing*) have a second Accusative (Predicative) in agreement with the Object:

> Sōcratēs tōtīus sē mundī cīvem arbitrābātur. CICERO.
> *Socrates used to consider himself a citizen of the whole world.*

Note.—The Accusative is used as the Subject of an Infinitive to form a Substantival Clause (**238–240**).

> Sōlem fulgēre vidēmus: *We see that the sun shines.*

35 Some Verbs of *teaching*, *asking*, *concealing* (doceō, *teach*; flāgitō, postulō, poscō, *demand*; rogō, *ask*; ōrō, *pray*; cēlō, *conceal*), take two Accusatives, one of the Person, the other of the Thing:

> Racilius prīmum mē sententiam rogāvit. CICERO.
> *Racilius asked me my opinion first.*

> Prīmus ā Raciliō sententiam rogātus sum.
> *I was the first to be asked my opinion by Racilius.*

Note 1.—In the Passive, the Accusative of the Thing is occasionally kept.
Note 2.—Quaerō, petō, take Ablative of the Person with ā or ab (instead of the Accus. of the Person): hoc ā tē petō, *this I ask of you.*

---

36 **Place to which Motion** is directed is in the Accusative: eō Rōmam, *I go to Rome.*

37 ### Cognate Accusative

Many Verbs, which are otherwise Intransitive, take an Accusative containing the same idea as the Verb and often etymologically connected with it:

> Fortūna lūdum īnsolentem lūdit. HORACE.
> *Fortune plays an insolent game.*

38 ### Adverbial Accusative

The **Accusative of Respect** is used with Verbs and Adjectives:

> Tremit artūs. VIRGIL.   Nūdae lacertōs. TACITUS.
> *He trembles in his limbs.*   *Bare as to the arms.*

THE DATIVE CASE

139 The Dative expresses relations which in English are generally indicated by the prepositions *to* and *for*.

Dative of the Indirect Object

140 The Dative of the Indirect Object is used:

(1) With Transitive Verbs of *giving, telling, showing, saying, promising*, which take also an Accusative of the Direct Object:

Tibi librum sollicitō damus aut fessō. HORACE.
We give you a book when you are anxious or weary.

Saepe tibi meum somnium nārrāvī. CICERO.
I have often told you my dream.

141 (2) With some Verbs which are Intransitive in Latin, although their English equivalents are transitive. Such Verbs have the Dative as their only Object. Instances of such Verbs are:

crēdō, *believe*; fīdō, *trust*; ignōscō, *pardon*; imperō, *command*; īrāscor, *to be angry with*; pāreō, *obey*; serviō, *serve*; suādeō, *advise*.

Imperat aut servit collēcta pecūnia cuique. HORACE.
Money amassed rules or serves every man.

Imperiō pārent. CAESAR.   Parce piō generī. VIRGIL.
They obey the command.   *Spare a pious race.*

Note.—These Verbs contain the ideas of *being helpful to, favourable to*, &c.

142 Dēlectō, *delight*, iuvō, *help*, laedō, *harm*, gubernō, regō, *govern, control*, iubeō, *command*, take an Accusative:

Multōs castra iuvant. HORACE.   Animum rege. HORACE.
The camp delights many.   *Rule the temper.*

Temperō, moderor, *control, restrain*, sometimes take an Accusative, instead of the Dative:

Hic moderātur equōs quī nōn moderābitur īrae.
This man, who will not control his temper, controls horses.

143 (3) With Adjectives implying *nearness, fitness, likeness, help, kindness, trust, obedience*, or any opposite idea:

Hortus ubi et tēctō vīcīnus iūgis aquae fōns. HORACE.
Where is a garden, and near to the house a fount of flowing water.

Hominī fidēlissimī sunt equus et canis. PLINY.
The horse and dog are most faithful to man.

144 When compounded with any Preposition (except per, praeter, trāns), or with re-, or with the Adverbs bene, male, satis:

(a) Many Intransitive Verbs which took neither the Accusative of the Direct Object, nor the Dative of the Indirect Object, now take a Dative of the Indirect Object:

> Subvēnistī hominī iam perditō. CICERO.
> *You have come to the help of a man already lost.*
>
> Nūllus in orbe sinus Baiīs praelūcet amoenīs. HORACE.
> *No bay in the world outshines the pleasant Baiae.*

(b) Many Transitive Verbs which took only an Accusative of the Direct Object may now take also a Dative of the Indirect Object:

> Mūnītiōnī Labiēnum praefēcit. CAESAR.
> *He put Labienus in charge of the fortification.*

Dative of Advantage or Reference

45 The person (or thing) for whose advantage or disadvantage something is done, or in reference to whom something happens, is indicated by the Dative Case:

> Sīc vōs nōn vōbīs mellificātis, apēs! VIRGIL.
> *Thus ye make honey not for yourselves, O bees!*
>
> Nōn sōlum nōbīs dīvitēs esse volumus. CICERO.
> *We do not wish to be rich for ourselves alone.*

46 The **Dative of the Possessor,** with esse, is used when emphasis is laid on the thing possessed, not on the possessor.

> Est mihī plēnus Albānī cadus. HORACE.
> *I have a cask full of Alban wine* (lit. *there is to me*).

47 The **Predicative Dative,** accompanied by a Dative of Reference, is used instead of the Nominative or Accusative of a Noun or Adjective in the Predicate after (1) sum, *I am, I serve as,* (2) verbs like habeō, dūcō, meaning *I consider as, reckon as*:

> Exitiō est avidum mare nautīs. HORACE.
> *The greedy sea is a destruction to sailors.*

47a The **Dative of Purpose** expresses the end in view:

> Equitātum auxiliō Caesarī mīsērunt. CAESAR.
> *They sent the cavalry as a help to Caesar.*

THE ABLATIVE CASE

148 The Ablative expresses relations which in English are generally indicated by the Prepositions, *from, with, by, in.*

A. Pure Ablatives

149 The **Ablative of Separation** is used (*a*) with Verbs meaning *to keep away from, free from, deprive, lack;* (*b*) with Adjectives of similar meaning, as līber, *free;* (*c*) with the Adverb procul, *far from:*

Populus Athēniēnsis Phōciōnem patriā pepulit. NEPOS.
The Athenian people drove Phocion from his country.

149a The **Ablative of Origin** is used with Verbs, chiefly Participles, implying descent or origin:

Atreus, Tantalō prōgnātus, Pelope nātus. CICERO.
Atreus, descended from Tantalus, and son of Pelops.

150 The **Ablative of Comparison** is used with Comparative Adjectives and Adverbs instead of quam (*than*) with a Nominative or Accusative:

Nihil est amābilius virtūte. CICERO.
Nothing is more amiable than virtue.

Note 1.—The Ablative expresses the point 'from which' the comparison begins: *starting with virtue,* &c.
Note 2.—If other cases than the Nom. or Accus. are involved in the comparison, the quam construction *must* be used.

B. Ablatives of Association

151 The **Ablative of Association** is used with Verbs and Adjectives denoting *plenty, fulness, possession:* abundō, *abound,* dōnō, *present,* praeditus, *endowed with* (**169**):

Vīlla abundat gallīnā, lacte, cāseō, melle. CICERO.
The farm abounds in poultry, milk, cheese, honey.
Iuvenem praestantī mūnere dōnat. VIRGIL.
He presents the youth with a noble gift.

152 The **Ablative of Quality** is used with an Adjective in agreement (**171**):

Senex prōmissā barbā, horrentī capillō. PLINY.
An old man with long beard and rough hair.

153 Ablative of Respect or Specification:

Et corde et genibus tremit. HORACE.
It trembles both in heart and knees.

Note 1.—In the phrases nātū maior, *older,* nātū minor, *younger,* nātū is an Ablative of Respect.
Note 2.—Dignus, *worthy,* indignus, *unworthy,* dignor, *deem worthy,* are followed by an Ablative or Respect:

Dignum laude virum Mūsa vetat morī. HORACE.
A man worthy of praise the Muse forbids to die.

---

154 The **Ablative of the Manner** in which something happens or is done has an Adjective in agreement with it; *or* it follows the Preposition **cum**, *with*:

> Iam veniet tacitō curva senecta pede. OVID.
> *Presently bent old age will come with silent foot.*
>
> Magnā cum cūrā atque dīligentiā scrīpsit. CICERO.
> *He wrote with great care and attention.*

155 The **Ablative Absolute** is a phrase consisting of a Noun in the Ablative Case and a Participle (or another Noun or Adjective) in agreement with it: it is called Absolute because in construction the Noun and Participle are independent of the rest of the Sentence:

> Rēgibus exāctīs cōnsulēs creātī sunt. LIVY.
> *Kings having been abolished, consuls were elected.*
>
> Nīl dēspērandum Teucrō duce. HORACE.
> *There must be no despair, Teucer being leader.*

C. Instrumental Ablatives

156 The **Ablative of the Agent** indicates the *person* by whom something is done, and it is accompanied by the Preposition **ā, ab.**

157 The **Ablative of Instrument or Means** indicates the *instrument* by which something is done, and it is not accompanied by a Preposition:

> Hī iaculīs, illī certant dēfendere saxīs. VIRGIL.
> *These strive to defend with javelins, those with stones.*

158 The Deponent Verbs **fungor**, *perform*, **fruor**, *enjoy*, **vēscor**, *feed on*, **ūtor**, *use*, **potior**, *possess oneself of* (169), unlike their English equivalents, are Intransitive and take an Ablative of Instrument:

> Numidae ferīnā carne vēscēbantur. SALLUST.
> *The Numidians used to feed on the flesh of wild animals.*

159 An Ablative of Instrument is used with **frētus (sum)**, **nītor**, *I support myself, lean on*, **opus, ūsus (est)**, *there is need*, **cōnsistō**, *consist of*:

> Iuvenis quī nītitur hastā. VIRGIL.
> *A youth who leans on a spear.*

160 The **Ablative of the Cause** is used with Adjectives, Passive Participles, and Verbs (especially those denoting a mental state):

> Ōdērunt peccāre malī formīdine poenae. HORACE.
> *The bad hate to sin through fear of punishment.*

161 An **Ablative of the Measure of difference** is joined with Comparatives and Superlatives, and, rarely, with Verbs:

> Sōl multīs partibus maior est quam lūna. CICERO.
> *The sun is a great deal larger than the moon.*

162 The **Ablative of Price** is used with Verbs and Adjectives of *buying* and *selling*:

> Servum quadrāgintā minīs ēmit.
> *He bought a slave for (with) forty minae.*

D. The Ablative of Place and Time; the Locative Case

163 The **Ablative of Place and Time** includes the uses of the old Locative case which expressed the place where, or the time at which, an action occurred.

> For the Ablative indicating 'Place Where', see **178**.
> For the Ablative indicating 'Time at Which', see **183**.

The true **Locative Case** is used:

(*a*) In the singular of names of towns and small islands of the First and Second Declensions (and occasionally of the Third):

> Rōmae; Corcȳrae; Corinthī; Carthāginī.

(*b*) In some special forms:

> domī; bellī; mīlitiae; rūrī; humī; vesperī.

THE GENITIVE CASE

164 The Genitive is used to define or complete the meaning of another Noun on which it depends.   It is also used with certain Verbs and Adjectives.

A. Genitives of Definition

165 The **Appositional Genitive** depends on another Noun which it qualifies like a Noun in Apposition:

> Vōx voluptātis.   Nōmen rēgis.
> *The word pleasure.*   *The name of king.*

Note.—But the name of a city is always placed in Apposition: urbs Rōma, *the city of Rome.*

---

166 The **Attributive** or **Descriptive Genitive** defines the Noun on which it depends by mentioning its content or material:

> Acervus frūmentī.   Obtortī circulus aurī.
> *A pile of corn.*   *A chain of twisted gold.*

167 The **Genitive of the Author:**

> Ea statua dīcēbātur esse Myrōnis. CICERO.
> *That statue was said to be Myro's.*

168 Verbs and Adjectives of *accusing, condemning, convicting,* or *acquitting* take a Genitive of the fault or crime:

> Alter latrōciniī reus, alter caedis convictus est. CICERO.
> *The one was accused of robbery, the other was convicted of murder.*

169 Verbs and Adjectives implying *want* and *fulness*, especially egeō, indigeō, *want*, impleō, *fill*, potior, *get possession of*, plēnus, *full*, often take a Genitive; (**151, 158**):

> Virtūs plūrimae exercitātiōnis indiget. CICERO.
> *Virtue needs very much practice.*

> Rōmānī sīgnōrum potītī sunt. SALLUST.
> *The Romans get possession of the standards.*

B. Possessive Genitive

170

> Rēgis cōpiae. CICERO.　　Contempsī Catilīnae gladiōs. CICERO.
> *The king's forces.*　　*I have braved the swords of Catiline.*

C. Genitive of Quality

171 The **Genitive of Quality** has an Adjective in agreement:

> Ingenuī vultūs puer ingenuīque pudōris. JUVENAL.
> *A boy of noble countenance and noble modesty.*

172 **Genitives of Value**, magnī, parvī, plūrimī, minimī, nihilī, are used with Verbs of *valuing*; the Genitives tantī, quantī, plūris, minōris, are also used with Verbs of *buying* and *selling*, but not to express a definite price:

> Voluptātem sapiēns minimī facit.
> *The wise man accounts pleasure of very little value.*

D. Genitive of the Whole, or Partitive Genitive

173 The Genitive of a Noun of which a part is mentioned is called a Genitive of the Whole, or a Partitive Genitive.

> Sīc partem maiōrem cōpiārum Antōnius āmīsit. CICERO.
> *Thus Antony lost the greater part of his forces.*

> Multae hārum arborum meā manū sunt satae. CICERO.
> *Many of these trees were planted by my hand.*

E. The Subjective and Objective Genitive

174 The terms Subjective and Objective Genitives refer primarily to two different relations of the Genitive to a Noun on which it depends. Thus amor patris, *the love of a father*, may mean either 'the love felt *by* a father' (where patris is a Subjective Genitive, *cf.* pater amat), or 'the love felt *for* a father' (where patris is an Objective Genitive, *cf.* amō patrem).

175 An Objective Genitive is used with Verbal Substantives, Adjectives (especially those in -āx) in which a verbal notion is prominent, and Participles which have the meaning of *love, desire, hope, fear, knowledge, skill, power.*

With Substantives:

> Erat īnsitus mentī cognitiōnis amor. CICERO.
> *Love of knowledge had been implanted in the mind.*

With Adjectives and Participles:

> Avida est perīculī virtūs. SENECA.
> *Valour is greedy of danger.*

> Quis famulus amantior dominī quam canis? COLUMELLA.
> *What servant is fonder of his master than the dog is?*

F. Genitive with Verbs

176 Most Verbs of *remembering, forgetting*, meminī, reminīscor, oblīvīscor, usually take the Genitive:

> Animus meminit praeteritōrum. CICERO.
> *The mind remembers past things.*

Note 1.—The Accusative is sometimes used instead of the Genitive, with these Verbs.

> Nam modo vōs animō dulcēs reminīscor, amīcī. OVID.
> *For now I remember you, O friends, dear to my soul.*

Note 2.—Recordor, *I remember*, almost always takes the Accusative.

177 The Adjectives corresponding to these Verbs, memor, immemor, always take a Genitive:

> Omnēs immemorem beneficī ōdērunt. CICERO.
> *All hate one who is forgetful of a kindness.*

Two Verbs of *pitying*, misereor, miserēscō, take a Genitive:

> Arcadiī, quaesō, miserēscite rēgis. VIRGIL.
> *Take pity, I entreat, on the Arcadian king.*

> Nīl nostrī miserēre. VIRGIL.
> *You pity me not at all.*

Note.—Miseror, commiseror take an Accusative.

PLACE, TIME, AND SPACE

Place

178 Place where anything is or happens is generally in the Ablative Case with the Preposition **in**; sometimes (especially in Poetry), when an Adjective qualifies the Substantive, the Preposition is omitted:

>Castra sunt in Italiā contrā rempūblicam collocāta. CICERO.
>*A camp has been formed in Italy against the Republic.*

>Celsā sedet Aeolus arce. VIRGIL.
>*Aeolus is seated on his high citadel.*

179 Place whence there is motion is expressed by the Ablative with **ā, ab, ex,** or **dē**:

>Ex Asiā trānsīs in Eurōpam. CURTIUS.
>*Out of Asia you cross into Europe.*

180 Place whither is expressed by the Accusative with a Preposition:

>Caesar in Italiam magnīs itineribus contendit. CAESAR.
>*Caesar hastened by long marches into Italy.*

181 In names of **towns** and **small islands,** also in **domus** and **rūs, Place where, whence,** or **whither** is expressed by a Case without a Preposition:

(a) **Place where,** by the Locative:

>Quid Rōmae faciam? JUVENAL.   Is habitat Mīlētī. TERENCE.
>*What am I to do at Rome?*   *He lives at Miletus.*

>Philippus Neāpolī est, Lentulus Puteolīs. CICERO.
>*Philip is at Naples, Lentulus at Puteoli.*

>Sī domī sum, forīs est animus; sīn forīs sum, animus est domī. PLAUTUS.
>*If I am at home, my mind is abroad; if I am abroad, my mind is at home.*

(b) **Place whence,** by the Ablative:

>Dēmarātus fūgit Tarquiniōs Corinthō. CICERO.
>*Demaratus fled from Corinth to Tarquinii.*

(c) **Place whither,** by the Accusative:

Rēgulus Carthāginem rediit. CICERO.
Regulus returned to Carthage.

Vōs īte domum; ego rūs ībō.
Go ye home; I will go into the country.

Note.—With names of towns, **ad** is used to mean *to the neighbourhood of:*
ventum est ad Cannās. LIVY.

182 The road by which one goes is in the Ablative:

Ībam forte Viā Sacrā. HORACE.
I was going by chance along the Sacred Way.

Time

183 Time at which, in answer to the question When? is expressed
by the Ablative: hieme, *in winter*; sōlis occāsū, *at sunset*:

Ego Capuam vēnī eō ipsō diē. CICERO.
I came to Capua on that very day.

184 Time within which, by the Ablative:

Quicquid est bīduō sciēmus. CICERO.
Whatever it is, we shall know in two days.

185 Time during which, by the Accusative:

Rōmulus septem et trīgintā rēgnāvit annōs. LIVY.
Romulus reigned thirty-seven years.

Space

186 Space traversed is expressed by the Accusative:

Mīlia tum prānsī tria rēpimus. HORACE.
Then having had luncheon we crawl three miles.

186a Space which lies between is expressed by the Accusative or
Ablative:

Reliquae legiōnēs magnum spatium aberant. CAESAR.
The rest of the legions were at a long distance.

187 Space of Measurement, answering the questions *How high? How
deep? How broad? How long?* is generally expressed by the
Accusative:

Erant mūrī Babylōnis ducēnōs pedēs altī. PLINY.
The walls of Babylon were two hundred feet high.

PREPOSITIONS

188 With **Accusative**:

ante, apud, ad, adversus, *before, near, to, towards,*
clam, circum, circā, citrā, cis, *unknown to, around, about, this side of,*
contrā, inter, ergā, extrā, *against, between, towards, outside of,*
īnfrā, intrā, iuxtā, ob, *beneath, within, beside, on account of,*
penes, pōne, post, and praeter, *in the power of, behind, after, along,*
prope, propter, per, secundum, *near, on account of, through, next to,*
suprā, versus, ultrā, trāns; *above, towards, beyond, across;*
Add super, subter, sub and in, Add *over, underneath, under, into,*
When '*motion*' 'tis, not '*state*', When they mean '*motion*', not '*state*'.
they mean.

189 With **Ablative**:

ā, ab, absque, cōram, dē, *by, from, without, in the presence of, from,*
palam, cum, and ex, and ē, *in sight of, with, out of,*
sine, tenus, prō, and prae: *without, as far as, for, before:*
Add super, subter, sub and in, Add *over, underneath, under, in,*
When '*state*', not '*motion*', 'tis When they mean '*state*', not '*motion*'.
they mean.

Clam, *secretly*, and palam, *openly*, are used by classical prose writers mainly as adverbs, very rarely indeed as prepositions.

IMPERSONAL VERBS

CASE CONSTRUCTION

190 The following Verbs of *feeling* take an Accusative of the person with a Genitive of the cause: **miseret, piget, paenitet, pudet, taedet**:

> Miseret tē aliōrum, tuī tē nec miseret nec pudet. PLAUTUS.
> *You pity others, for yourself you have neither pity nor shame.*

191 **Libet, licet, liquet, contingit, convenit, ēvenit, expedit,** take a Dative (sometimes with an Infinitive as the Impersonal Subject):

> Nē libeat tibi quod nōn licet. CICERO.
> *Let not that please you which is not lawful.*

192 With **rēfert,** *it concerns*, *it matters*, the person concerned is expressed by the fem. Ablative singular of a Possessive Adjective (meā, tuā, &c.); the degree of concern by Adverbs of degree (magnopere, &c.) or by a Genitive of value (parvī, &c.), or by an Adverbial Accusative (multum, plūs, quid, &c.):

> Quid meā rēfert cui serviam?   PHAEDRUS.
> *What does it matter to me whom I serve?*

193 **Interest,** *it concerns*, *it is of importance*, has the same construction as rēfert; in addition, it may take a Genitive of the person or thing concerned:

> Interest omnium rēctē facere.   CICERO.
> *It is for the good of all to do right.*
>
> Et tuā et meā interest tē valēre.   CICERO.
> *It is of importance to you and to me that you should be well.*

Note.—The use of meā, tuā with interest is due to the analogy of rēfert.

PASSIVE CONSTRUCTION

194 When a sentence is changed from the Active to the Passive form:

The Object of a Transitive Verb becomes the Subject; the Subject becomes the Agent in the Ablative with the Preposition ā or ab:

> Numa lēgēs dedit.   CICERO.   *Numa gave laws.*
> Lēgēs ā Numā datae sunt.   *Laws were given by Numa.*

195 Intransitive Verbs are used in the Passive only in an Impersonal construction:

The Personal Subject of an Intransitive Verb (1) becomes the Agent:

> Nōs currimus: Ā nōbīs curritur: *We run.*

or (2) is not referred to at all:

> Conclāmātum 'ad arma', concursumque ad mūrōs est.   LIVY.
> *They raised the shout 'To arms!' and rushed to the walls.*

PRONOUNS AND PRONOMINAL ADJECTIVES

196 The Personal Pronouns as the Subjects of Verbs are generally not expressed; but they are sometimes added for emphasis.

The **Reflexive Pronoun, Sē,** is used to refer:
(*a*) to the subject of the Simple Sentence or Subordinate Clause in which it stands;
(*b*) to the subject of a Principal Sentence, if the Subordinate Clause in which it stands represents something in the mind of that subject;
(*c*) to the subject of a Verb of *saying* which introduces Ōrātiō Oblīqua.

197 The Possessive Adjective **suus** is used like **sē**:

Sentit animus sē vī suā, nōn aliēnā, movērī. Cicero.
The mind feels that it moves by its own force, not by that of another.

Note.—Sometimes, when no ambiguity is likely, suus refers in a Simple Sentence to something other than the grammatical subject:

Suīs flammīs dēlēte Fidēnās. Livy.
With its own flames destroy Fidenae.

---

198 Eius, *his*, never refers to the Subject of the Sentence:

Chīlius tē rogat, et ego eius rogātū. Cicero.
Chilius asks you, and I at his request.

199 Hic and ille are often used in contrast:

Quōcumque adspiciō, nihil est nisi pontus et āěr,
flūctibus hic tumidus, nūbibus ille mināx. Ovid.

*Whithersoever I look, there is nought but sea and sky,
the one threatening with clouds, the other heaped with billows.*

200 Ipse, *self*, is of all the three Persons, with or without a Personal Pronoun: ipse ībō, *I shall go myself.*

201 Of the **Indefinite Pronouns and Adjectives,** the most definite is **quīdam,** the least so **quis.**

Aliquis means *some one*: dīcat aliquis, *suppose some one to say*; sī vīs esse aliquis, *if you wish to be somebody.*

202 Quidam means a *certain person* (often known, but not named):

accurrit quīdam, *a certain man runs up.*

203 Quisquam (Substantive),
     Ullus (Adjective): } *any at all,*

are generally used after a negative word, or a question expecting a negative answer:

> Nec vērō necesse est ā mē quemquam nōminārī.   CICERO.
> *Nor indeed is it necessary for anyone to be named by me.*

> Nōn ūllus arātrō dignus honōs.   VIRGIL.
> *Not any due honour (is given) to the plough.*

204 Quīvīs, quīlibet, *any you like:*

> Nōn cuivīs hominī contingit adīre Corinthum.   HORACE.
> *It does not happen to every man to go to Corinth.*

205 Quisque, *each* (severally), is often used with sē, suus:

> Sibi quisque habeant quod suum est.   PLAUTUS.
> *Let them have each for himself what is his own.*

206 Uterque, *each* (of two), can be used with the Genitive of Pronouns; but with Substantives it agrees in Case:

> Uterque parēns.   OVID.   Utrōque vestrum dēlector.   CICERO.
> *Both father and mother.*   *I am delighted with each of you.*

207 Uter, *which* (of two), is Interrogative:

> Uter utrī īnsidiās fēcit?   CICERO.
> *Which of the two laid an ambush for the other?*

208 Alter, *the one, the other* (of two), *the second*, is the Demonstrative of uter: alter ego, *a second self*:

> Quicquid negat alter, et alter.   HORACE.
> *Whatever the one denies, so does the other.*

209 Alius, *another* (of any number), *different*:

> Fortūna nunc mihi, nunc aliī benigna.   HORACE.
> *Fortune, kind now to me, now to another.*

THE VERB INFINITE

210 The parts of the Verb Infinite have some of the uses of Verbs, some of the uses of Nouns.

THE INFINITIVE

211 The **Infinitive** as a Verb has Voices (Active and Passive) and Tenses (Present, Past, and Future), it governs Cases, and is qualified by Adverbs; as a Noun it is neuter, and indeclinable, used only as Nominative or Accusative.

212 The **Infinitive** as a **Nominative** may be the Subject of Impersonal Verbs, or of Verbs used impersonally.

> Iuvat īre et Dōrica castra vidēre. VIRGIL.
> *It is pleasant to go and view the Doric camp.*
>
> Dulce et decōrum est prō patriā morī. HORACE.
> *To die for one's country is sweet and seemly.*

213 The **Infinitive** is often one of the two **Accusatives** depending on Factitive Verbs.

> Errāre, nescīre, dēcipī, et malum et turpe dūcimus. CICERO.
> *To err, to be ignorant, to be deceived, we deem both unfortunate and disgraceful.*

214 The **Prolative Infinitive** (so called, *cf.* **124**) is used as the Direct Object of:

> Verbs of *possibility, duty, habit; wishing, daring; beginning, ceasing,* &c.; *knowing, learning, teaching.*
>
> Solent diū cōgitāre quī magna volunt gerere. CICERO.
> *They are wont to reflect long who wish to do great things.*

GERUND AND GERUNDIVE

215 The Gerund is a Verbal Noun, active in meaning; it has no plural. The Gerundive is a Verbal Adjective, passive in meaning.

216 The **Accusative** of the Gerund follows some Prepositions, usually ad, sometimes ob, inter:

> Ad bene vīvendum breve tempus satis est longum. CICERO.
> *For living well a short time is long enough.*
>
> Mōrēs puerōrum sē inter lūdendum dētegunt. QUINTILIAN.
> *The characters of boys show themselves in their play.*

217 The **Genitive** of the Gerund depends on some Abstract Substantives, and on Adjectives which take a Genitive:

Ars scrībendī discitur.
The art of writing is learnt.

Cupidus tē audiendī sum.   CICERO.
I am desirous of hearing you.

218 The **Dative** of the Gerund is used with a few Verbs, Adjectives, and Substantives, implying *help, use, fitness*:

Pār est disserendō.   CICERO.
He is equal to arguing.

Operam legendō dat.
He gives attention to reading.

219 The **Ablative** of the Gerund expresses Instrument or Cause; or it follows one of the Prepositions in, ab, dē, ex:

Fugiendō vincimus.
We conquer by flying.

Dē pugnandō dēlīberant.
They deliberate about fighting.

220 If a Verb is Transitive, its **Gerundive** is used in preference to its Gerund with an Accusative:

Ad pācem petendam vēnērunt.   LIVY.
They came to seek peace.

Note 1.—The Gerundive is passive: 'ad pācem petendam' properly means 'for peace which is to be sought'; but it is equivalent in meaning to the active 'for seeking peace'.
Note 2.—The Dative of the Gerundive is used to show purpose:

Comitia rēgī creandō.   LIVY.
An assembly for electing a king.

221 The Gerundive is also used to express that something *must* or *ought to be done*, the Dative of the Agent being expressed or understood.

222 If the Verb is **Intransitive** the nominative neuter of its Gerundive is used impersonally in this sense:

Eundum est.
One must go.

Mihi eundum est.
I must go.

223 If the Verb is **Transitive** its Gerundive is used in this sense:

Caesarī omnia ūnō tempore erant agenda.   CAESAR.
All things had to be done by Caesar at one time.

SUPINES

224 The Supines in -um and -ū are the Accus. and Dat. (or Abl.) cases of a Verbal Noun.

225 The **Supine** in **-um** is used after Verbs of motion, expressing purpose:

> Lūsum it Maecēnās, dormītum ego. HORACE.
> *Maecenas goes to play, I to sleep.*

With the Infinitive **īrī,** used impersonally, it forms the Future Passive Infinitive:

> Aiunt urbem captum īrī.
> *They say that the city will be taken.*

Note.—Literally, *they say there is a going to take the city.*

---

226 The **Supine** in **-ū** is used with some Adjectives, such as facilis, dulcis, turpis, and the Substantives fās, nefās:

> Hoc fās est dictū.   Lībertās, dulce audītū nōmen. LIVY.
> *It is lawful to say this.*   *Freedom, a name sweet to hear.*

ADVERBS

227 **Adverbs** show how, when, and where the action of the Verb takes place; they also qualify Adjectives or other Adverbs: rēctē facere, *to do rightly*; hūc nunc venīre, *to come hither now*; facile prīmus, *easily first.*

Many words are both Adverbs and Prepositions, as ante, *before*, post, *after.*

228 The **Negative Adverbs** are **nōn, haud, nē.**

Nōn, *not,* simply denies:

> Nivēs in altō marī nōn cadunt. PLINY.
> *No snow falls on the high seas.*

Haud, *not,* negatives other Adverbs, Adjectives, and a few Verbs of *knowing* and *thinking*:

> Rēs haud dubia.   Haud aliter.
> *No doubtful matter.*   *Not otherwise.*

Nē negatives the Imperative and (generally) Subjunctives of Will and Desire.

> Tū nē cēde malīs, *Do not yield to misfortunes*; Nē trānsierīs Hibērium, *Do not cross the Ebro*; Nē vīvam, sī scio, *May I not live, if I know.*

CONJUNCTIONS AND INTERJECTIONS

229 **Conjunctions** connect words, sentences and clauses.

230 (1) **Co-ordinative Conjunctions** connect two or more Nouns in the same Case:

> Mīrātur portās strepitumque et strāta viārum. VIRGIL.
> *He marvels at the gates and the noise and the pavements.*

Or they connect two or more Simple Sentences:

> Caesar properāns noctem diēī coniūnxerat neque iter intermīserat.
> CAESAR.
> *Caesar in his haste had joined night to day and had not broken his march.*

231 (2) **Subordinative Conjunctions** join Dependent Clauses to the Principal Sentence.   (See Complex Sentence.)

Co-ordination

232 Two or more sentences joined together by Co-ordinative Conjunctions are said to be **Co-ordinate Sentences,** and each is independent of the other in construction:

> Gȳgēs ā nūllō vidēbātur, ipse autem omnia vidēbat. CICERO.
> *Gyges was seen by no one, while he himself saw all things.*

INTERJECTIONS

233 **Interjections** are apart from the construction of the sentence:

> Ō fōrmōse puer, nimium nē crēde colōrī. VIRGIL.
> *O beautiful boy, trust not too much to complexion.*
>
> Ō fortūnātam Rōmam! CICERO.
> *O fortunate Rome!*
>
> Ēn ego vester Ascanius! VIRGIL.
> *Lo here am I your Ascanius!*
>
> Ei miserō mihi!   Vae victīs! LIVY.
> *Alas! wretched me.*   *Woe to the vanquished!*

Note.—The sentence in which an Interjection occurs often contains a Vocative, or Accusative, or Dative (of Reference).

QUESTION

234 (*a*) **Direct Single Questions** are introduced by:

> nōnne, implying the answer *yes*.
> num, implying the answer *no*.
> -ne, with no implication.

>> Canis nōnne similis lupō est? CICERO.
>> *Is not a dog like a wolf?*

>> Num negāre audēs? CICERO.　　Potesne dīcere? CICERO.
>> *Do you venture to deny?*　　*Can you say?*

235 (*b*) **Direct Alternative Questions** are introduced by:

> utrum ⎱
> -ne 　⎰ ... an, anne (*or*) an nōn (*or not*).

>> Haec utrum abundantis an egentis sīgna sunt? CICERO.
>> *Are these the tokens of one who abounds or lacks?*

>> Rōmamne veniō, an hīc maneō, an Arpīnum fugōi? CICERO.
>> *Do I come to Rome, or stay here, or flee to Arpinum?*

THE COMPLEX SENTENCE

236 A **Complex Sentence** consists of a Principal Sentence with one or more Subordinate Clauses.

237 Subordinate Clauses are divided into:

I. Substantival.　　　**II. Adverbial.**　　　**III. Adjectival.**

I. SUBSTANTIVAL CLAUSES

238 A **Substantival Clause** is an Indirect Statement, Command, Wish or Question.

239 It stands, like a Noun, in some case-relation (generally that of Nominative or Accusative) to the Verb of the Principal Sentence.

240   **1. Indirect Statement**

I. An **Infinitive with Subject Accusative** is the most usual form
of Indirect Statement.   It may stand:

   (a) As **Subject** of an Impersonal Verb, or of **est** with an
      Abstract Substantive or Neuter Adjective:

      Cōnstat lēgēs ad salūtem cīvium inventās esse.   CICERO.
      It is agreed that laws were devised for the safety of citizens.

   (b) As **Object,** after Verbs of *saying, thinking, feeling, perceiv-*
      ing, knowing, believing, denying:

      Dēmocritus dīcit innumerābilēs esse mundōs.   CICERO.
      Democritus says that there are countless worlds.

II. A Clause introduced by **ut** and having its Verb in the
Subjunctive is used (a) as Subject with Impersonal Verbs or
phrases which express fact or occurrence; (b) as the Object of
faciō and its compounds.

     (a) Fit ut nēmō esse possit beātus.   CICERO.
        It is the case that no one can be happy.

     (b) Quae rēs ut commeātus portārī posset efficiēbat.   CAESAR.
        And this had the result that provisions could be brought.

III. A Clause introduced by **quod** (*the fact that*) and having its
Verb in the **Indicative** is used (a) as the Subject of Impersonal
Verbs or phrases where a fact is stressed; (b) as the Object of
Verbs like **addō, mittō, omittō, praetereō,** and Verbs of *rejoicing*
and *grieving*; (c) in apposition to a preceding Substantive:

     (a) Bene mihi ēvenit quod mittor ad mortem.   CICERO.
        It is well for me that I am sent to death.

     (b) Adde quod īdem nōn hōram tēcum esse potes.   HORACE.
        Besides, you cannot keep your own company for an hour.

     (c) Hōc praestāmus maximē ferīs, quod loquimur.   CICERO.
        We excel beasts most in this respect, that we speak.

241 ## 2. Indirect Command or Prohibition

Indirect Commands or Prohibitions are Substantival Clauses which correspond to Simple Sentences in which the Imperative or the Subjunctive of Will is used. The Conjunctions are **ut** (positive) and **nē** (negative). Here belong clauses depending on Verbs *implying an act of the will,* as: *command, entreat; exhort, urge; persuade, induce; resolve; take care; permit.*

> Helvētiīs persuāsit ut exīrent. CAESAR.
> *He persuaded the Helvetii to depart.*
>
> Cūrā et prōvidē ut nēquid eī dēsit. CICERO.
> *Take care and see that he lack nothing.*

242 ## 3. Indirect Question

An Indirect Question is a Substantival Clause dependent upon a Verb of *asking, enquiring, telling, knowing,* or the like. It is introduced by an Interrogative Pronoun or Particle and its Verb is **Subjunctive:**

> Quaesīvit salvusne esset clipeus. CICERO.
> *He asked whether his shield was safe.*
>
> Fac mē certiōrem quandō adfutūrus sīs. CICERO.
> *Let me know when you will be here.*

243 ## II. ADVERBIAL CLAUSES

1. **Consecutive Clauses** define the consequence of what is stated in the Principal Sentence. They are introduced by **ut**, *so that*, and their Verb is in the Subjunctive. The negative Adverb is **nōn**.

> Nōn sum ita hebes ut istud dīcam. CICERO.
> *I am not so stupid as to say that.*

2. **Final Clauses** express the aim or purpose of the action of the Principal Sentence. They are introduced by **ut**, *in order that* (if negative, by **nē, ut nē**), and the Verb is Present or Imperfect Subjunctive:

> Veniō ut videam.   Abiī nē vidērem.
> *I come that I may see.*   *I went away that I might not see.*

3. **Causal Clauses** assign a reason for the statement made in the Principal Sentence.

When the speaker vouches for the reason, **quod, quia, quoniam,**

quandō are used with the Indicative; otherwise the Verb is Subjunctive.

> Adsunt proptereā quod officium sequuntur; tacent quia perīculum metuunt. CICERO.
> *They are present because they follow duty; they are silent because they fear danger.*

A Causal Clause introduced by **cum**, *since*, has its Verb in the Subjunctive even though the reason is vouched for:

> Quae cum ita sint, ab Iove pācem ac veniam petō. CICERO.
> *Since these things are so, I ask of Jupiter peace and pardon.*

4. **Temporal Clauses** define the time when anything has happened, is happening, or will happen.

Ubi, ut, *when,* **postquam,** *after,* **simulac, cum prīmum,** *as soon as,* **quotiēns,** *whenever,* are generally used with the Indicative:

> Olea ubi mātūra erit quam prīmum cōgī oportet. CATO.
> *When the olive is ripe, it must be gathered as soon as possible.*

Cum, referring to a Past action, is, with a few exceptions, used with the Imperfect or Pluperfect Subjunctive.

> Cum Pausaniās dē templō ēlātus esset, cōnfestim animam efflāvit. NEPOS.
> *When Pausanias had been carried down from the temple, he immediately expired.*

5. **Conditional Statements** consist of (i) a Clause introduced by **sī** (*if*), **nisi** (*unless*), containing a preliminary condition, called the **Protasis,** and (ii) a Principal Sentence, containing the consequence, which is called the **Apodosis.**

The condition in the sī-clause may be:
(1) open, *i.e.* nothing is implied about the fulfilment or probability of fulfilment;
(2) only conceded as a supposition and may or may not be fulfilled;
(3) one that is contrary to known facts.

In **Type I** the Indicative is used in the Protasis and generally in the Apodosis.

> Sī valēs, bene est. CICERO.
> *If you are in good health, all is well.*

In **Type II** the Present (or Perfect) Subjunctive is used:

> Hanc viam sī asperam esse negem, mentiar. CICERO.
> *If I were to deny that this road is rough, I should lie.*

In **Type III** the Imperfect or Pluperfect Subjunctive is used:

> Sī ad centēnsimum annum vīxisset, senectūtis eum suae paenitēret? CICERO.
> *If he had lived to his hundredth year, would he be regretting his old age?*

6. Concessive Clauses are introduced by etsī, etiamsī, tametsī, *even if*; quamquam, quamvīs, licet, *although*.

Etsī, etiamsī, tametsī take the Indicative or the Subjunctive, like sī-clauses.

> Etiamsī tacent, satis dīcunt. CICERO.
> *Even if they are silent, they say enough.*

> Etiamsī nōn is esset Caesar quī est, tamen ōrnandus vidērētur. CICERO.
> *Even if Caesar were not what he is, yet he would be considered worthy of honour.*

Quamquam is used with the Indicative:

> Quamquam festīnās, nōn est mora longa. HORACE.
> *Although you are in haste, the delay is not long.*

Quamvīs, licet are used with the Subjunctive:

> Quamvīs nōn fuerīs suāsor, approbātor fuistī. CICERO.
> *Although you did not make the suggestion, you have given your approval.*

7. Clauses of Proviso are introduced by dum, dummodo, modo, *provided that*. The Verb is in the Subjunctive, and the negative nē.

> Magnō mē metu liberābis dummodo mūrus intersit. CICERO.
> *You will free me from a great fear, provided a wall is between us.*

8. In **Clauses of Comparison** the action or fact of the Principal Sentence is compared:

(i) with something asserted as a fact (Indicative):

> Ut brevissimē dīcī potuerunt, ita ā mē dicta sunt. CICERO.
> *These things have been said by me as briefly as possible.*

(ii) with a supposed condition (Subjunctive):

> Tamquam sī claudus sim, cum fūstī est ambulandum. PLAUTUS.
> *I must walk with a stick as if I were lame.*

III. ADJECTIVAL CLAUSES

244 When the **Relative quī** introduces a clause which merely states a **fact** about the Antecedent, the Verb is **Indicative**:

> Est in Britanniā flūmen quod appellātur Tamesis. CAESAR.
> *There is in Britain a river which is called the Thames.*

But when the Relative introduces a Consecutive, Final, or Causal Clause, corresponding to the Adverbial Clauses with similar meaning, the Verb is **Subjunctive**.

> Ea est Rōmāna gēns quae victa quiēscere nesciat. LIVY.
> *The Roman race is such that it knows not how to rest quiet under defeat.*

SEQUENCE OF TENSES

245 The general rule for the Sequence of Tenses is that a Primary Tense in the Principal Sentence is followed in the Subordinate Clause by a Primary Tense (Present, Future, Perfect [e.g. = *I have asked*], Future Perfect), a Historic Tense by a Historic Tense (Imperfect, Perfect [e.g. = *I asked*], Pluperfect).

SIMPLE AND PRINCIPAL SENTENCES IN ŌRĀTIŌ OBLĪQUA

246 A speech reported indirectly as the object of a Verb of *saying* is called **Ōrātiō Obliqua**.

247 **Statements and Exclamations** are expressed by an Accusative and Infinitive.

Direct	*Indirect*
Rōmulus urbem condidit.	(Nārrant:) Rōmulum urbem condidisse.
Romulus founded the city.	

248 **Commands, Prohibitions, and Wishes** are expressed by the Subjunctive:

Īte, inquit, creāte cōnsulēs ex plēbe.	(Hortātus est:) īrent, creārent cōnsulēs ex plēbe.
Go, he says, and elect consuls from the plebs.	*He exhorted them to go and elect consuls from the plebs.*

249 **Real Questions** (*i.e.* those to which an answer is expected) are expressed by the **Subjunctive**:

Quid agis? inquit. Cūr nōn anteā pugnam commīsistī?	Quid ageret? Cūr nōn anteā pugnam commīsisset?
What are you about?	*Why have you not joined battle before?*

Rhetorical Questions (*i.e.* those which do not expect an answer) are expressed by an Accusative and Infinitive:

Cūr ego prō hominibus ignāvīs sanguinem profūdī?

Cūr sē prō hominibus ignāvis sanguinem profūdisse?

Why have I shed my blood for cowards?

250 Adverbial and Adjectival Clauses have their Verbs in the Subjunctive:

Maiōrum quibus ortī estis reminīsciminī.

(Dīxit): maiōrum quibus ortī essent reminēscerentur.

Remember the ancestors from whom you are sprung.

251 When the Verb of *saying* is Third Person (as usually is the case):

Ego, nōs; meus, noster	become	sē; suus.
Tū, vōs; tuus, vester	become	ille, illī; illīus, illōrum.
Hic	becomes	ille *or* is.

Since the Reflexives **sē, suus** may refer to the subject of a Verb other than the Verb of *saying*, ambiguity is possible.
Sometimes **ipse** makes the distinction clear:

(Rogāvit): quid tandem verērentur aut cūr dē suā virtūte aut dē ipsīus dīligentiā dēspērārent? CAESAR.

What cause had they to fear, or why did they despair either of their own bravery or of his carefulness?

52

Direct Statement	Indirect Statement
Cum Germānīs Aeduī semel atque iterum armīs contendērunt; magnam calamitātem pulsī accēpērunt, omnem nōbilitātem, omnem equitātum āmīsērunt. Sed peius victōribus Sēquanīs quam Aeduīs victīs accidit; proptereā quod Ariovistus, rēx Germānōrum, in eōrum fīnibus cōnsēdit, tertiamque partem agrī Sēquanī, quī est optimus tōtīus Galliae, occupāvit. Ariovistus barbarus, īrācundus, temerārius est; nōn possunt eius imperia diūtius sustinērī.	Locūtus est prō Aeduīs Divitiacus: Cum Germānīs Aeduōs semel atque iterum armīs contendisse; magnam calamitātem pulsōs accēpisse, omnem nōbilitātem, omnem equitātum āmīsisse. Sed peius victōribus Sēquanīs quam Aeduīs victīs accidisse; proptereā quod Ariovistus, rēx Germānōrum, in eōrum fīnibus cōnsēdisset, tertiamque partem agrī Sēquanī, quī esset optimus tōtīus Galliae, occupāvisset. Ariovistum esse barbarum, īrācundum, temerārium, nōn posse eius imperia diūtius sustinērī.

The Aedui have repeatedly fought with the Germans; they have been defeated and have suffered great misfortune; they have lost all their nobles and all their cavalry. But worse has befallen the conquering Sequani than the conquered Aedui, for Ariovistus, king of the Germans, has settled in their dominions and occupied a third part of their territory, which is the best in all Gaul. Ariovistus is barbarous, passionate and violent; his commands can no longer be endured.

Divitiacus said on behalf of the Aedui: 'That the Aedui had fought repeatedly with the Germans; that, having been defeated, they had suffered great misfortune (and) had lost all their nobles, all their cavalry. But that worse had befallen the conquering Sequani than the conquered Aedui, for Ariovistus, king of the Germans, had settled in their dominions and had occupied a third part of their territory, which was the best in all Gaul. That Ariovistus was barbarous, passionate and violent; and that his commands could no longer be endured.'

253   Direct Command

Vestrae prīstinae virtūtis et tot secundissimōrum proeliōrum retinēte memoriam, atque ipsum Caesarem, cuius ductū saepenumerō hostēs superāvistis, praesentem adesse exīstimāte.

Keep in mind your former valour and your many successful battles, and imagine that Caesar, under whose leadership you so often overcame your foes, is himself present.

Indirect Command

Labiēnus mīlitēs cohortātus ut suae prīstinae virtūtis et tot secundissimōrum proeliōrum retinērent memoriam, atque ipsum Caesarem, cuius ductū saepenumerō hostēs superāssent, praesentem adesse exīstimārent, dat sīgnum proeliī.

Labienus, having exhorted the soldiers to keep in mind their former valour and their many successful battles, and to imagine that Caesar, under whose leadership they had so often overcome their foes, was himself present, gives the signal for battle.

RULES OF QUANTITY

54

I. General Rules of Quantity

1. A syllable is long if it ends:
   (*a*) In a long vowel or diphthong: scrī-bae.
   (*b*) In two consonants or a compound consonant: dant, dux.
   (*c*) In a single consonant followed by a syllable beginning with a
   consonant: mul-tōs.

2. All other syllables are short.

Note 1.—Poets often divide a combination of Plosive and Liquid between
two syllables, so that the first syllable is long even if it contains a short
vowel: pat-ris, teneb-rae, trip-lex. 'h' and 'u' in 'qu-' do not count as
consonants.

Note 2.—A vowel or diphthong is short before another vowel or h (in the
same word): proavus, trahō, praeesse. Exceptions are: certain parts of
fīō and some cases of Fifth Declension words in -iēs.

Note 3.—In Greek words a long vowel or diphthong keeps its length: āēr,
Aenēās, Enyō, Melibœus.

Note 4.—Compounds of iaciō, though written iniciō, adiciō, have their
first syllable long as if pronounced inyiciō, adyiciō.

Note 5.—Consonant-i between vowels was pronounced as a double
consonant, and the first syllable of words like eius, huius, is long.

---

3. A syllable is called doubtful when it is found in poetry to be sometimes
long, sometimes short: Dīāna, fidēī, rēī, and genitives in -ius, as illīus.

4. The quantity of a stem syllable is kept, as a rule, in compounds and
derivatives: cadō occidō, ratus irritus, flūmen flūmineus; but exceptions to
this rule are numerous.

55

II. Rule for Monosyllables

Most monosyllables are long: dā, dēs, mē, vēr, sī, sīs, sōl, nōs, tū, vīs,
mūs.

Exceptions:

Substantives: cor, fel, lac, mel, os (*bone*), vas (*surety*), vir.
Pronouns: is, id, qua (*any*), quis, quid, quod, quot, tot.
Verbs: dat, det, it, scit, sit, stat, stet, fit, fac, fer, es (from sum).
Particles: ab, ac, ad, an, at, bis, cis, et, in, nec, ob, per, pol, sat, sed,
sub, ut, vel,
and the enclitics -ne, -que, -ve.

56

III. Rules for Final Syllables

1. A final is short.
   Exceptions.—Ablatives of decl. 1, mēnsā, bonā; Vocative of Greek
   names in ās, Aenēā; and of some in ēs, Anchīsā; Indeclinable Numerals,
   trīgintā; Imperatives of conj. 1, amā (but puta); most Particles in a;
   frūstrā, intereā (but ita, quia, short).

2. E final is short: legĕ, timētĕ, carērĕ.
   Exceptions.—Ablatives of decl. 5, rē, diē, with the derivatives quārē, hodiē. Cases of many Greek nouns; also famē. Adverbs formed from Adjectives; miserē; also ferē, fermē (but benĕ, malĕ, facĭlĕ, impūnĕ, temerĕ, short). Imperatives of conjugation 2. monē (but cavĕ is doubtful). Also the interjection ohē.

3. I final is long: dīcī, plēbī, dolī.
   Exceptions.—Vocatives and Datives of Greek nouns: Chlŏrĭ, Thyrsidĭ; but Datives sometimes long: Parĭdī. Particles; sīcubi, nēcubi, nisi, quasi. Mihĭ, tibĭ, sibĭ, ubĭ, and ibĭ are doubtful.

4. O final is long: virgō, multŏ, iuvō.
   Exceptions.—Duŏ, egŏ, modŏ, citŏ, and three verbs: putŏ, sciŏ, nesciŏ. In the Silver Age final o was often shortened in Verbs and Nouns.

5. U final is long: cantū, dictū, diū.

6. A vowel before final c is long: illīc; except dōnec.

7. A vowel before final l, d, t is short: Hannibal, illud, amāvit.

8. A vowel before final n is short: Īlion, agmen.
   Exceptions.—Many Greek words: Hymēn, Ammōn.

9. A vowel before final r is short: calcar, amābitur, Hector.
   Exceptions.—Many Greek words: āēr, crātēr; and compounds of pār: dispār, impār.

10. Final -as is long: terrās, Menalcās.
    Exceptions.—Greek nouns of decl. 3. Arcăs (gen. -adis), and acc. pl. lampadăs; anăs, *a duck.*

11. Final -es is long: nūbēs, vidērēs.
    Exceptions.—Cases of Greek nouns: Arcadĕs, Nāiadĕs. Nominatives of a few substantives and adjectives with dental stems in -et, -it, or -id: segĕs, pedĕs, obsĕs, dīvĕs (but abiēs, ariēs, pariēs); also penĕs. Compounds of es: adĕs, potĕs.

12. Final -is short: dīcerĭs, ūtilĭs, ēnsĭs.
    Exceptions.—Datives and Ablatives in īs, including grātīs, forīs. Accusatives in īs: nāvīs; some Greek nouns in īs: Salamīs. Sanguĭs, pŭlvĭs, are doubtful. 2nd Personal Singular Present Indicative conjugation 4, audīs; compounds of vīs, sīs, *e.g.* quīvīs, possīs; also velīs, mālīs, nōlīs. 2nd Personal Singular Perfect Subjunctive, amāverīs.

13. Final -os is long: ventōs, custōs, sacerdōs.
    Exceptions.—Greek nominative and genitive in os (*os*): Dēlŏs, Arcadŏs; also compŏs, impŏs, exŏs.

14. Final -us is short: holŭs, intŭs, amāmŭs.
    Exceptions.—Nominatives from long stems of decl. 3 are long: virtūs, tellūs, incūs, iuventūs; genitive singular and nominative and accusative plural of decl. 4: artūs, gradūs; and a few Greek words: Dīdūs, Sapphūs (genitive).

15. The Greek words chlamys, chelys, Tĭphys, Erīnys have the final syllable short and the vocative ending y.

APPENDIX I

MEMORIAL LINES ON THE GENDER OF LATIN SUBSTANTIVES

I. General Rules
   The Gender of a Latin Noun
   by meaning, form, or use is shown.

1. A Man, a name of People and a Wind,
   River and Mountain, Masculine we find:
   Rōmulus, Hispānī, Zephyrus, Cōcȳtus, Olympus.

2. A Woman, Island, Country, Tree,
   and City, Feminine we see:
   Pēnelopē, Cyprus, Germānia, laurus, Athēnae.

3. To Nouns that cannot be declined
   The Neuter Gender is assigned:
   Examples fās and nefās give
   And the Verb-Noun Infinitive:
   Est summum nefās fallere:
   Deceit is gross impiety.

Common are: sacerdōs, dux,	*priest (priestess), leader*
vātēs, parēns et coniūnx,	*seer, parent, wife (husband)*
cīvis, comes, custōs, vindex,	*citizen, companion, guard, avenger*
adulēscēns, īnfāns, index	*youth (maid), infant, informer*
iūdex, testis, artifex,	*judge, witness, artist*
praesul, exsul, opifex,	*director, exile, worker*
hērēs, mīles, incola,	*heir (heiress), soldier, inhabitant*
auctor, augur, advena,	*author, augur, new-comer*
hostis, obses, praeses, āles,	*enemy, hostage, president, bird*
patruēlis et satelles,	*cousin, attendant*
mūniceps et interpres,	*burgess, interpreter*
iuvenis et antistes,	*young person, overseer*
aurīga, prīnceps: add to these	*charioteer, chief*
bōs, damma, talpa, serpēns, sūs,	*ox (cow), deer, mole, serpent, swine*
camēlus, canis, tigris, perdix, grūs	*camel, dog, tiger, partridge, crane.*

II. Special Rules for the Declensions

Decl. 1 (Ā- Stems).

Rule.—Feminine in First *a*, *ē*,
      Masculine *ās*, *ēs* will be.

Exc.   Nouns denoting Males in *a*
    are by meaning *Māscula*:
    and Masculine is found to be
    Hadria, *the Adriatic Sea.*

Decl. 2 (O- Stems).

Rule.—O-Nouns in *us* and *er* become
      Masculine, but Neuter *um*.

Exc.   Feminine are found in *us*,
    alvus, Arctus, carbasus,   *paunch, Great Bear, linen*
    colus, humus, pampinus,   *distaff, ground, vine-leaf*
    vannus: also trees, as pirus;   *winnowing-fan, pear-tree*
    with some jewels, as sapphīrus;   *sapphire*
    Neuter pelagus and vīrus.   *sea, poison*
    Vulgus Neuter commonly,   *common people*
    rarely Masculine we see.

Decl. 3 (Consonant and I- Stems).

Rule 1.—Third-Nouns Masculine prefer
      endings *ō*, *or*, *ŏs*, and *er*;
      add to which the ending *ĕs*,
      if its Cases have increase.

Exc. (*a*)   Feminine exceptions show
    Substantives in *dō* and *gō*.
    But ligō, ōrdō, praedō, cardō,   *spade, order, pirate, hinge*
    Masculine, and Common margō.   *margin*

    (*b*)   Abstract Nouns in *iō* call
    Fēminīna, one and all:
    Masculine will only be
    things that you may touch or see,
    (as curculiō, vespertīliō,   *weevil, bat*
    pugiō, scīpiō, and pāpiliō)   *dagger, staff, butterfly*
    with the Nouns that number show,
    such as terniō, sēniō.   *3, 6*

    (*c*)   Ēchō Feminine we name: *echo*
    carō (carnis) is the same.   *flesh*

(*d*) Aequor, marmor, cor decline   *sea, marble, heart*
Neuter; arbor Feminine.   *tree*

(*e*) Of the Substantives in *ŏs*,
Feminine are cōs and dōs: *whetstone, dowry*
while, of Latin Nouns, alone
Neuter are os (ossis), *bone*,
and ōs (ōris), *mouth*: a few
Greek in *os* are Neuter too.*

(*f*) Many Neuters end in *er*,
siler, acer, verber, vēr,   *withy, maple, stripe, spring*
tūber, ūber, and cadāver,   *hump, udder, carcase*
piper, iter, and papāver.   *pepper, journey, poppy*

(*g*) Feminine are compēs, teges,   *fetter, mat*
mercēs, merges, quiēs, seges,   *fee, sheaf, rest, corn*
though their Cases have increase:
with the Neuters reckon aes.   *copper*

Rule 2.—Third-Nouns Feminine we class
ending *is, x, aus*, and *ās*,
s to consonant appended,
ēs in flexion unextended.

Exc. (*a*) Many Nouns in *is* we find
to the Masculine assigned:
amnis, axis, caulis, collis,   *river, axle, stalk, hill*
clūnis, crīnis, fascis, follis,   *hind-leg, hair, bundle, bellows*
fūstis, ignis, orbis, ēnsis,   *bludgeon, fire, orb, sword*
pānis, piscis, postis, mēnsis,   *bread, fish, post, month*
torris, unguis, and canālis,   *stake, nail, canal*
vectis, vermis, and nātālis,   *lever, worm, birthday*
sanguis, pulvis, cucumis,   *blood, dust, cucumber*
lapis, cassēs, Mānēs, glīs.   *stone, nets, ghosts, dormouse*

(*b*) Chiefly Masculine we find,
sometimes Feminine declined,
callis, sentis, fūnis, fīnis,   *path, thorn, rope, end*
and in poets torquis, cinis.   *necklace, cinder*

(*c*) Masculine are most in *ex*:
Feminine are forfex, lēx,   *shears, law*
nex, supellex: Common, pūmex   *death, furniture, pumice*
imbrex, ōbex, silex, rumex.   *tile, bolt, flint, sorrel*

* As melos, *melody*; epos, *epic poem*.

(d) Add to Masculines in *ix*,
   fornix, phoenix, and calix.   *arch, —, cup*

(e) Masculine are adamās,   *adamant*
   elephās, mās, gigās, ās: *elephant, male, giant, as*
   vas (vadis) Masculine is known,   *surety*
   vās (vāsis) is a Neuter Noun.   *vessel*

(f) Masculine are fōns and mōns,   *fountain, mountain*
   chalybs, hydrōps, gryps, and pōns,   *iron, dropsy, griffin, bridge*
   rudēns, torrēns, dēns, and cliēns,   *cable, torrent, tooth, client*
   fractions of the ās, as triēns.   *four ounces*
   Add to Masculines tridēns,   *trident*
   oriēns, and occidēns,   *east, west*
   bidēns (*fork*); but bidēns (*sheep*),
   with the Feminines we keep.

(g) Masculine are found in *ēs*
   verrēs and acīnacēs.   *boar, scimitar*

Rule 3.—Third-Nouns Neuter end *a, e,*
   ar, ur, us, c, l, n, and *t.*

Exc. (a) Masculine are found in *ur*
   furfur, turtur, vultur, fūr.   *bran, turtle-dove, vulture, thief*

(b) Feminine in *ūs* a few
   keep, as virtūs, the long *ū*:   *virtue*
   servitūs, iuventūs, salūs,   *slavery, youth, safety*
   senectūs, tellūs, incūs, palūs.   *old-age, earth, anvil, marsh*

(c) Also pecus (pecudis)   *beast*
   Feminine is Gender is.

(d) Masculine appear in *us*
   lepus (leporis) and mūs.   *hare, mouse*

(e) Masculines in *l* are mūgil,   *mullet*
   cōnsul, sāl, and sōl, with pugil.   *consul, salt, sun, boxer*

(f) Masculine are rēn and splēn,   *kidney, spleen*
   pecten, delphīn, attagēn.   *comb, dolphin, grouse*

(g) Feminine are found in *ōn*
   Gorgōn, sindōn, halcyōn.   *Gorgon, muslin, kingfisher*

Decl. 4 (U- stems).

Rule.—Masculines end in *us*: a few
   are Neuter nouns, that end in *ū.*

Exc.	Women and trees are Feminine, with acus, domus, and manus, tribus, Īdūs, porticus.	*needle, house, hand,* *tribe, the Ides, porch*

Decl. 5 (Ē-Stems).

Rule.—Feminine are Fifth in *ēs*,
Except merīdiēs and diēs.   *noon, day*

Exc. Diēs in the Singular
    Common we define;
    But its Plural cases are
    always Masculine.

Exceptions to the Rules for the Genitive Plural of the Third Declension

IMPARISYLLABIC NOUNS WITH GEN. PLUR. IN -ium	PARISYLLABIC NOUNS WITH GEN. PLUR. IN -um
-ium in Plural Genitive os (ossis) and ās (assis) give; so mās, mūs, nox, and glīs and līs, with **frōns** (frontis) and **frōns** (frondis); and fōns, mōns, pōns, and glāns and gēns, urbs too and trabs, stirps, arx and dēns, and ars and pars, and sors and mēns. To these add often, dōs, parēns, lār, īnfāns, serpēns, and rudēns; bidēns too, and aetās (aetātis) with others ending in -ās (ātis).	-um in Plural Genitive pater, māter, frāter give, with accipiter and canis, senex, sēdēs, iuvenis; generally too, mēnsis, vātēs, apis, volucris.

List of Prepositions

With Accusative:

Ante, apud, ad, adversus, Clam, circum, circā, citrā, cis, Contrā, inter, ergā, extrā, Infrā, intrā, iuxtā, ob, Penes, pōne, post, and praeter.	Prope, propter, per, secundum, Suprā, versus, ultrā, trāns; Add super, subter, sub and in, When '*motion*' 'tis, not '*state*', they mean.

With Ablative:

Ā, ab, absque, cōram, dē, Palam, cum, and ex, and ē, Sine, tenus, prō, and prae:	Add super, subter, sub and in, When '*state*', not '*motion*', 'tis they mean.

APPENDIX II

A SELECT LIST OF COMPOUND VERBS

COMPOUNDS OF sum (§81)

	Present	Infinitive	Perfect*	Supine*	
(ā, ab)	absum	abesse	āfuī		am absent
(ad)	adsum	adesse	adfuī		am present
(dē)	dēsum	dēesse	dēfuī		am wanting
(in)	īnsum	inesse	īnfuī		am in
(inter)	intersum	interesse	interfui		am between
	interest	interesse			it concerns
(ob)	obsum	obesse	obfuī		am in the way, hinder
(prae)	praesum	praeesse	praefuī		am in command
(prō)	prōsum	prōdesse	prōfuī		am of use
(sub)	subsum	subesse			am under, near
(super)	supersum	superesse	superfuī		am still alive

COMPOUNDS OF dō (§99a)

	Present	Infinitive	Perfect*	Supine*	
(circum)	circumdō	circumdare	circumdedī	circumdatum	surround
(vēnum)	vēnumdō	vēnumdare	vēnumdedī	vēnumdatum	sell
(ā, ab)	abdō	abdere	abdidī	abditum	put away, hide
(ad)	addō	addere	addidī	additum	put to, add
(cum)	condō	condere	condidī	conditum	found
	crēdō	crēdere	crēdidī	crēditum	trust, believe
(dē)	dēdō	dēdere	dēdidī	dēditum	surrender
(ē, ex)	ēdō	ēdere	ēdidī	ēditum	put forth, utter

Similarly: (per) perdō, ruin, lose; (prae) praeditus, *endowed with*; (prō) prōdō, *betray*; (re) reddō, *give back, return*; (sub) subdō, *subdue*; (vēnum) vēndō, *sell*.

COMPOUNDS OF stō (§109)

	Present	Infinitive	Perfect*	Supine*	
(circum)	circumstō	circumstāre	circumstetī		stand round
(cum)	cōnstō	cōnstāre	cōnstitī		be well-known, cost
(ob)	obstō	obstāre	obstitī		thwart, withstand
(prae)	praestō	praestāre	praestitī	praestatum	be superior, show

* When the space for Perfect or Supine is left blank, it means that the Verb in question has none in good use.

COMPOUNDS OF agō (§111)

	Present	Infinitive	Perfect	Supine	
(circum)	circumagō	circumagere	circumēgī	circumāctum	*drive round*
(per)	peragō	peragere	perēgī	perāctum	*accomplish*
(ad)	adigō	adigere	adēgī	adāctum	*thrust, urge to an act*
(cum)	cōgō	cōgere	coēgī	coāctum	*compel*
(dē)	dēgō	dēgere			*spend time, live*
(prō)	prōdigō	prōdigere	prōdēgī		*squander, waste*
(re)	redigō	redigere	redēgī	redāctum	*drive back*

COMPOUNDS OF emō (*take*) *buy* (§111)

(ad)	adimō	adimere	adēmī	adēmptum	*take away*
(cum)	coemō	coemere	coēmī	coēmptum	*buy up*
(inter)	interimō	interimere	interēmī	interemptum	*take away, destroy*
(per)	perimō	perimere	perēmī	perēmptum	*destroy*
(cum)	cōmō	cōmere	cōmpsī	cōmptum	*adorn*
(dē)	dēmō	dēmere	dēmpsī	dēmptum	*take away*
(prō)	prōmō	prōmere	prōmpsī	prōmptum	*bring out*
(sub)	sūmō	sūmere	sūmpsī	sūmptum	*take*

COMPOUNDS OF habeō

	habeō	habēre	habuī	habitum	*have*
(ad)	adhibeō	adhibēre	adhibuī	adhibitum	*apply*
(dē)	dēbeō	dēbēre	dēbuī	dēbitum	*owe*
(prae)	praebeō	praebēre	praebuī	praebitum	*held forth, proffer*
(prō)	prohibeō	prohibēre	prohibuī	prohibitum	*check, prevent*

COMPOUNDS OF eō (*go*) (§102)

(ā, āb)	abeō	abīre	abiī	abitum	*go away*
(ad)	adeō	adīre	adiī	aditum	*approach*

Similarly: **(ex ē) exeō**, *go out*; **(in) ineō**, *go into*; **(inter) intereō**, *perish*; **(per) pereō**, *pass away, die*; **(praeter) praetereō**, *go by or past*; **(re) redeō**, *go back*; **(trāns) trānseō**, *go across*; **(vēnum) vēneō**, *go for sale, be sold*.

COMPOUNDS OF ferō, *bear* (§101)

	Present	Infinitive	Perfect	Supine	
(ad)	afferō	afferre	attulī	allātum	*bring to*
(ā, ab)	auferō	auferre	abstulī	ablātum	*take away*
(dē)	dēferō	dēferre	dētulī	dēlātum	*carry down*
(dis)	differō	differre	distulī	dīlātum	*carry different ways*
(ob)	offerō	offerre	obtulī	oblātum	*bring before, offer*
(re)	referō	referre	rettulī	relātum	*bring back*

COMPOUNDS OF iaciō, *throw* (§111)

(ā, ab)	abiciō	abicere	abiēcī	abiectum	*throw away*
(ad)	adiciō	adicere	adiēcī	adiectum	*throw to*

Similarly: (cum) coniciō, *throw together, unite*; (dis) disiciō, *throw asunder*; (in) iniciō, *throw into*.

COMPOUNDS OF faciō, *do, make* (§111)

(ad)	afficiō	afficere	affēcī	affectum	*do something to*

Similarly: (cum) cōnficiō, *complete, accomplish*; (dē) dēficiō, *forsake, revolt*; (inter) interficiō, *kill*; (per) perficiō, *finish*; (prae) praeficiō, *appoint to command*; (prō) proficiō, *advance, make progress*; (re) reficiō, *remake, restore*; (prō) proficiscor, *make (put) oneself forward, set out*.

calefaciō	calefacere	calefēcī	calefactum	*make hot, heat*
patefaciō	patefacere	patefēcī	patefactum	*lay open*

COMPOUNDS OF capiō, *take* (§111)

(ad)	accipiō	accipere	accēpī	acceptum	*receive*

Similarly: (cum) concipiō, *take hold of*; (dē) dēcipiō, *deceive*; (ē, ex) excipiō, *catch*; (in) incipiō, *begin*; (sub) suscipiō, *take up*.

COMPOUNDS OF cadō, *fall*

	cadō	cadere	cecidī	cāsum	*fall*
(ad)	accidō	accidere	accidī		*fall upon, happen*
(in)	incidō	incidere	incidī	incāsum	*fall into*
(ob)	occidō	occidere	occidī	occāsum	*fall down*
(re)	recidō	recidere	reccidī	recāsum	*fall back*

COMPOUNDS OF caedō, *cut*

	Present	Infinitive	Perfect	Supine	
	caedō	caedere	cecīdī	caesum	*cut*
(in)	incīdō	incīdere	incīdī	incīsum	*cut into*
(ob)	occīdō	occīdere	occīdī	occīsum	*cut down, kill*

COMPOUNDS OF rapiō, *snatch* (§111)

| (ā, ab) | abripiō | abripere | abripuī | abreptum | *tear away* |

Similarly: **(ad) arripiō**, *snatch*; **(cum) corrīpiō**, *seize*; **(dis) dīripiō**, *tear asunder, plunder*; **(ē, ex) ēripiō**, *snatch away*.

COMPOUNDS OF regō, *rule* (§84)

| (ad) | arrigō | arrigere | arrēxī | arrēctum | *raise, rouse* |

Similarly: **(cum) corrigō**, *make straight*; **(ē, ex) ērigō**, *raise up, erect*.
Also: **(per) pergō**, *proceed*; **(sub) surgō**, *rise*; **(ex, per) expergīscor**, *begin to stretch oneself out, arouse oneself, wake*.

COMPOUNDS OF gradior, gradi, gressus sum, *step*

| (ad) | aggredior | aggredī | aggressus | | *approach, attack* |

Similarly: **dīgredior**, *go apart, separate*; **(prō) prōgredior**, *march forward*; **(re) regredior**, *turn back*.

COMPOUNDS OF currō, currere, cucurrī, cursum, *run*

| (ad) | accurrō | accurrere | accucurrī | accursum | *run to* |

Similarly: **(dē) dēcurrō**, *run down*; **(ē, ex) excurrō**, *run out*. (Also: **accurrī, dēcurrī, excurrī**.)

COMPOUNDS OF -speciō, *look*

| (ad) | aspiciō | aspicere | aspexī | aspectum | *look at* |
| (cum) | cōnspiciō | cōnspicere | conspexi | cōnspectum | *catch sight of* |

REMARKS ON re AND prō

re ('*back*'). This particle was in old Latin spelt **red**. The **d** has dropped off except in some compounds (*e.g.* **reddō, redigō, redeō**).

prō ('*forward*'). This preposition was in old Latin spelt **prōd**. The **d** has dropped off, as a rule, but has been retained before vowels (compare **prōsum** with **prōdesse** and **prōdigō** with **prōcumbō**).